When Tyranny Becomes Law

Zachary Richter

Patriot Lines Publishing—Merrill, WI
Paperback ISBN: 979-8-218-47652-6
eBook ISBN: 979-8-3303-4243-3
Library of Congress Control Number: 2024915237
Title: *When Tyranny Becomes Law*
Author: Zachary Richter
Digital distribution | 2024
Paperback | 2024

Dedication

I'd like to dedicate this book to my fellow Patriots who believe they are owed a better America, who believe America can and must be far better than it is today; and to those who fight and those who have fought to preserve the founding principles and spirt of our great nation from its conception up to today.

Table of Content

Prologue

Now, before your government became tyrannical, you and your people were probably in the minority and just wanted to live your lives the way you chose, free from oppressive control.

Your way of life became increasingly under attack, your culture shrinking while the opposing culture spreads.

The opposition takes the majority in government, military, media, big tech, academia, science, corporations, and even your source of employment.

The political elites in government, become more and more corrupt, becoming bought and paid for with bribes and now seek more control than ever before over you and your people. They use national emergencies, national defense, national guard, and the excuse of public safety as a weapon against you. The cultures decay leads to greater tampering in elections. The military no longer fights for what it used to. Big tech and the media are politically weaponized against you. The education system is weaponizing science and rewrites history to paint your people as the enemy and their people as the victims or the hero's. Corporations now fuel the opposing cultural movement by pandering to them through advertising. Your source of employment does the same and makes it increasingly difficult for you to provide for your family.

The opposition now has a bigger microphone and a larger audience to spread its propaganda while at the same time labeling what you say as lies, misinformation, and hate speech.

You become the target and are labeled a racist, a brainwashed hater of everyone different than you, an enemy, a problem, a noise in need of silencing. Your voice grows increasingly faint, and the oppositions voice shouts louder and louder. Your nation is almost unrecognizable from its founding.

The law becomes your last defensive hope for justice and equality, but soon, it becomes the last to fall victim to the corrupt power-hungry majority. You now have a one sided- partisan law, the greatest form of oppression. With no hope for any kind of a future life for you or your children, and no hope to regain lost freedoms; street incursions, general violence, and conflicts with law enforcement spike and the fuse for a rebellion has been lit.

But how did it come to this? With some nations it is too late to do anything about their inevitable demise as they give in to collective thinking and reject the existence of truth. With other nations there may still be hope. The United States of America for example is in a state that is like a train heading down a broken set of tracks at full speed. If Americans act now, there might be just enough time to repair the track or switch rails before her fate is sealed.

A French Resistance fighter smiles at a Nazi firing squad 1944

Soviet troops occupying Czechoslovakia 1968

"Tank man" Tiananmen Square Beijing 1989

The Great Proletarian Cultural Revolution 1966-1976

The Boston Massacre 1770

Lexington and Concord 1775

Chapter 1
AMERICA UNDER ATTACK

Is America great? If so, what makes it great? And should we not continuously encourage all that makes America great? If you ask an average citizen or a leftist, questions like this, they will miss the mark entirely every chance they are given. They might ramble on about our nation's problems in academics, healthcare, poverty, and the economy. This is a privileged response as we are only able to worry about, and capable of, improving these things because of how successful we have become. And we are successful as a result of what makes this nation great. There are many nations that are lucky if they even have schools or hospitals, lack any real economy, and everyone is in poverty. These are all important things, but this argument is missing the entire point of what makes America great. Or maybe they will answer stating that we are not any more free than any other nation in the world. In general, they're correct. But it's because of the left that we aren't as free as we used to be. Which is largely what this book is about. Our lost freedom, the rapid left leaning evolution of our government's politics and mindset of the general public, and if we don't do something about it soon, there won't be anything left of our freedom or founding principles to save.

Or maybe they will answer by regurgitating their college professors opinionated claims of America being founded on racism and other evils. Continuous babel exposing how little they understand or recognize the significance of, and how spoiled, brain washed and detached from reality they really are. They want us to be more like other, more progressively socialist nations. We don't want to have anything in common with those other nations. The people who came to this country were trying to get away from other nations and the same old way of thinking. The new way of thinking: freedom, independence, self-rule, human rights given to us by God and nature not by man. The idea that we can control our own destiny with lack of interference from those in power. Less government rather than more. Less about society, more about the individual. We are the mirrored opposite of the old world. That's what makes America great. That's what made America prosperous, and the generations that understood this, were the generations that made this country better. They were the people that built America.

At its birth, America was nothing. Add a hundred years, it becomes the world's leading economic and industrial powerhouse. Less than seventy years later, the world's sole superpower with nuclear capability. The rest of the world has had thousands of years to accomplish what past Americans did in less than two hundred. Common sense and minimal curiosity might cause one to ask how they did it. What was their economic system? What was their form of government? What type of character and values did the early American people have that contributed to such success. And the biggest question of all, are we about the same things today? Or are we pulling farther and farther away from those things and from our founding principles under the guise of progressivism?

A minor glimpse into the history of leftism in this country exposes the accelerating evolution of both major political parties and the nation's culture pulling farther left with less and less focus on what made this country great in the first place. Has each generation become more spoiled and self-serving than the previous? Have our traditional values been dismissed as outdated religious nonsense? Has the old world's influence grown more than our own? Have our schools and colleges stopped teaching what makes America great and started teaching anti-American ideology? Whatever the reason, there is no doubt a drastic shift in thinking and political party platforms. Fewer and fewer people are standing on principle and instead vote with their emotions and self-interest. Not many decades ago the democratic party's members had more in common with the modern republican party than modern democrats. Democrats of even twenty years hardly recognize their own party anymore. Many moderate democrats and independents are shifting over to the republican party. The republican party now has such a broad base, that many traditional republicans and American Patriots are starting to feel out of place or unheard. Meanwhile the leftist movement builds momentum as it decays our culture, society, and hands over many freedoms to the government.

Chapter 2
CORRUPTION

"Power tends to corrupt, and absolute power corrupts absolutely."

John Dalberg Acton

No one likes to feel powerless, and everyone likes to feel powerful. Power itself isn't necessarily the problem but human nature is. It's what we do when we have power. In the case of politicians in government, powerful positions attract those who lust after power. So, by nature, government is flawed, and government is a problem. However, by nature, human beings in general are flawed and therefore create problems. So, government is necessary but must be limited to the smallest and least powerful form.

<u>Small Government</u>

"That government is best which governs the least."

Thomas Jefferson

If you've ever had a job working for both a small business and a large corporation or government, you have a valuable perspective of the contrast between the two and have seen what works and what doesn't work in business. When a business grows large enough it usually has many business locations across a great distance. A hierarchy structure that allows it to implement changes across all its locations quickly and uniformly. But many problems occur with such a large authority structure. Poor communication is among the top reasons. The top can hand information down the chain of command, but the bottom can't hand information back up the chain as easily if at all. This is a system that needs to function like a body, with all parts communicating and coordinating with each other, but instead, the head can tell the feet to step forward, but the feet can't tell the head that they are about to trip. This makes for a very embarrassingly inefficient, dysfunctional, chaotic, and idiotic system. In the case of a small business, the communication chain is shorter, and the authority isn't unreachable for communications to come from the ground up. This allows for intelligent decision making, greater coordination, functionality, organization, and efficiency. The same applies for governments. Only in the case of government, power is another factor. Power that needs to be kept in check.

A smaller government means less power to be obtained by the government, meaning more power retained by the governed. A large government is rarely held accountable and therefore uncontrollable by the governed. Government must be as small and manageable by the governed as possible. But we have lost sight of what our founders wanted for us, and we have grown our government beyond our control, giving rise to the tyrannical Administrative State. Generally speaking, what is a state responsibility should be a local responsibility and what is a federal responsibility should be a state responsibility. The federal government should have as little responsibility as possible and as few employees as possible (not including military). We are rapidly losing our freedoms and must act now before it's too late.

"A body of men holding themselves accountable to nobody ought not to be trusted by anybody."

Thomas Paine

<u>Republic</u>

Our founders gave us the best possible form of government for our new nation. A Constitutional Republic. A Democracy would lead to a mob majority rule and oppress the minority. No wonder the left perpetuates the lie of claiming our nation is a democracy. The worst dictators in history took power with the sound of applause. They were placed into power by their own people. The majority have a track record of handing over the world on a silver platter as they are easily fooled and believe they will be catered to by their newfound hero.

"The purpose of the Constitution is to restrict the majority's ability to harm a minority."

James Madison

"It has been observed by an honorable gentleman, that a pure democracy, if it were practicable, would be the most perfect government. Experience has proved that no position in politics is more false than this. The ancient democracies, in which the people themselves deliberated never possessed one feature of good government. Their very character was tyranny; their figure deformity."

Alexander Hamilton

"Remember, Democracy never lasts long. It soon wastes, exhausts, and murders itself."

John Adams

"Give all power to the many, and they will oppress the few. Give all power to the few, and they will oppress the many."

Alexander Hamilton

Other forms of government have the same problem of balancing power among people. Our Constitutional Republic first distributes power to make the majority of power harder to obtain. Then lays out a series of checks and balances for the power of government and the power of the people. Starting with the constitution, consisting of amendments protecting citizens, and amendments limiting government power. Additional checks and balances include the separate branches of government, the representatives of the people with the representatives of the states, as well as the electoral college. And so, our government was purposely and precisely designed to limit both the power of government and the power of the majority over the minority as majority rule democracy only leads to oppression, less freedom, and big government, further leading to governments tyrannical control of everything. A Constitutional Republic is the only path to freedom. Our Republic has but one weakness, the integrity and virtue of its elected officials. This threat is cataclysmic if a majority of politicians lacking in character hold office simultaneously with a similar agenda. This is a result of a culture in decay. People of flawed character elect politicians of equally flawed character. Today our electoral college is under attack by the left. Should they dismantle or circumvent the electoral college in any way, our great Republic of freedom will be undone.

"If ever the time should come, when vain & aspiring men shall possess the highest seats in government, our country will stand in need of its experienced Patriots to prevent its ruin."

Samuel Adams

"The greatest danger to American freedom is a government that ignores the Constitution."

Thomas Jefferson

Corruption in the British parliament before the American Revolution was one of the main reasons for the American Revolutionary War. The colonists saw countless instances of Parliament corruption and injustice. One great example of this was the biggest reason for the Boston Tea Party. Like many, our education system probably taught you the colonists were just throwing a temper tantrum over taxes. In actuality, many in British parliament were heavily invested in the British East India Company and gave them special privileges which gave them a monopoly on selling tea in the colonies. A form of corruption that has always been in government and is found in our government today. The colonists were also outraged by the unconstitutional and childish behavior of the British parliament and king, by their constant attempts to discipline the colonies and demonstrate their authority over the colonists primarily through targeted taxation of imported goods.

We have seen our politicians ignore the constitution, ignore the fact that they were elected to serve the people and not themselves. They lie, cheat, and steal. They are bought and paid for by special interest groups. They are bought off by mafias, cartels, corporations and other nations' governments. They don't run for office to serve the people, they run to make themselves big easy money. The corrupt and wicked in power will do whatever it takes to stay in power and go to appalling lengths to keep good people out of power and out of their way. Even by means of influencing or rigging elections.

"If the representatives of the people betray their constituents, there is then no recourse left but in the exertion of that original right of self-defense which is paramount to all positive forms of government"

Alexander Hamilton

<u>Voter Corruption</u>

"When the people find that they can vote themselves money, that will herald the end of the republic."

Benjamin Franklin

Can the people themselves share responsibility for a corrupt government and dysfunctional society? We as a people have made many mistakes in the past. When a people are corrupt, then their culture and economy are corrupt. Then the government becomes even more corrupt. This creates a purely dysfunctional society. What creates corrupt people? Bad or selfish intentions create people lacking in morality, values and ability to contribute to society. These people vote for people like them and people who promise to give them what they want (such as money and to make every service free) instead of doing what's best for everyone or for our society and our nation's future.

We often don't seek out any balance of power between two entities of society by favoring the one that benefits the most people without any thought of bigger picture repercussions. Unions for instance, a noble start in helping people, now in many cases they have become tyrants of their own. From CRT to pedophiles to teachers that can't teach, if a poor teacher exists or one with unfavorable intentions is plaguing our children, they are overly protected by these teacher unions and the parents of these children become prisoners to these unions and are unable to defend or help their own children. Another example of a needed balance of power is between law enforcement and our citizens. In general, the higher government authorities may have too much power (and to little accountability) over citizens, while law enforcement on the local level, primarily in leftist leaning major cities (especially after the defund the police movement) now barely have enough authority to do their jobs.

We also filter out our options for candidates. If they're not rich or famous. If they don't sound or look the part. We are electing leaders without world experience straight out of college. We continue to elect politicians who have been in politics for decades and have lost touch with the real world. We are electing people with good acting skills, liars, cheaters, back stabbers, power hungry elitists who are disconnected from the realities of the commoner. Our founders intended our leaders to be elected for short time periods and be of the people so that they may be for the people.

Politicizing Tragedy

"You never want a serious crisis to go to waste."

Rahm Emanuel

Events of tragedy and misfortune seem to be occurring more frequently than ever before. Gun violence, school shootings, political unrest, disease, extreme weather, and natural disasters. And after every one of those, a corrupt politician has cold-heartedly sought to exploit the tragedy and the public's emotions to advance a political agenda and corrode or attack our freedoms. If there's an act of gun violence or a mass shooting, they waste no time attacking the 2nd amendment. If there's extreme weather or natural disasters, the left says it's global warming and try to increase regulations and outlaw technology. They blame Republicans in order to ensure their party members elections. If there's a disease, they choose security over freedom and anyone standing in their way is treated like a domestic terrorist. If it's political unrest they once again treat the opposition like domestic terrorists for being let into the capital building yet treat their own as saints, after having burned down half a city and placed it under occupation. They'll further use political unrest to villainize and attack their political opposition in power with lies and false accusations. Even if their political opposition is a siting U.S. President. Trial after trial, impeachment attempt after the next, indictment after indictment. The corruption and disease run deeper and is more severe than our worst conspiracy theories. Vladimir Putin when asked about the Trump prosecutions said, "As for the prosecution of Trump, for us what is happening in today's conditions, in my opinion, is good because it shows the rottenness of the American political system, which cannot pretend to teach others democracy. Everything that is happening with Trump is the persecution of a political rival for political reasons. That's what it is. And this is being done in front of the public of the United States and the whole world."

Governments have also been the cause of tragedy, and politicizing situations in order to do it. How many wars throughout history have been a result of ordinary people hating the ordinary people of their neighboring nations? Vs. How many pointless wars have been a result of a Corrupt and overly powerful government? How many human and innocent lives have been lost because of government? Even in just the last two hundred years we have seen actions of government including genocide, eugenics, forced organ harvesting, gain of function viral research, concentration camps, work camps, relocation camps, death marches, slavery, tyrannical oppression, starving their people, abuse and murder of the handicapped and mentally ill, chemical weapons, biological weapons, and nuclear weapons. *Governments did these things, not ordinary people.* The governments of the ancient world have done much worse.

"A desperate disease requires a dangerous remedy," Guy Fawkes

Distractions

"The truth is that all men having power ought to be mistrusted."

James Madison

Look over there not over here. Politicians have always been good at distracting people from things that would otherwise label them as the enemy, the threat or the problem. Leaders have done this throughout time. Roman emperors would use entertainment, festivals and military campaigns to distract the Roman people from the real problem; the emperor himself. Kings throughout the ages would follow this same model of distraction. Today, it's the same game just a different century. The distractions are much more diverse but serve the same purpose. National threats, war, disease, the economy, energy crises, global warming, natural disasters, terrorism. The list goes on and on. Our culture has also assisted our power-hungry politicians in keeping us distracted. Sex, drugs, entertainment, social media, technology. All keep us content and distracted. If we are distracted, we are content, and if we are content, we have no reason to become overly outraged with any news of the government or politician crossing that very fine line into infringing on our freedoms. With this the government consumes freedom, obtains power and grows too fat and large for anyone to stop it.

The government and our politicians also consume our hard-earned money and hope you don't notice. They will take your money and allocate it to a noble sounding cause such as "improving our national infrastructure" while they reallocate that money and use it for something completely unrelated that will help out their political friends and allies in an effort to advance their political agendas. The same is true with the use of government grants. The power of government to take our money and allocate it to whatever they want, is being used to perpetuate corruption and advance one political party's agendas. While we try to just survive, we don't notice how politicians seem to be thriving. That's _our_ money. If times get so bad, we start to take notice of what they are doing with our money. So, to further distract us, they feed us ideas of socialism to simultaneously distract us and trick us into giving them more power by convincing our most gullible, they will take care of us by giving us free money and services. Further accelerating their rise to power as every year we have less, and less freedom and the politicians have more and more power.

"Of more worth is one honest man to society, and in the sight of God, than all the crowned ruffians that ever lived."

Thomas Paine

<u>Friends of Corrupt Elitists</u>

"When once a Republic is corrupted, there is no possibility of remedying any of the growing evils but by removing the corruption and restoring its lost principles, every other correction is either useless or a new evil."

Thomas Jefferson

You scratch my back, I'll scratch yours. This is the foundational philosophy of all corrupt elites in government as they use their power to make themselves richer and more powerful. We'd like to believe our elected officials serve us, but they really serve themselves and worship money. If you want to know who the most powerful and corrupt person is, just follow the money. I'm not just talking about corporations buying politicians' legislative votes, Zucker-bucks, or Dark Money. I'm also talking about their paychecks. It's impossible to selflessly serve others when you're getting paid to do it. Doing "little favors" for those who write your paycheck is all too easy of a temptation for our "public servants." The Supreme Court Justices paychecks are determined by congress. Congress salaries are determined by the federal treasury. The trail continues on a very long crisscrossing intentionally confusing road that leads to the U.S. Office of Personnel Management (OPM) that determines salary of federal employees. Perhaps the person who is actually running the country can be found with ties to these paycheck writers.

With the lust for money and power that comes with men of flawed nature and character, it is no wonder and is also inevitable, that corrupt politicians and corrupt CEOs of corporations almost always find themselves getting all too friendly with each other. It's a simple business deal. Politicians have political power and want money; CEOs of corporations have money and want political power. Together they quickly evolve into an unstoppable stealthy force of tyranny.

"Fascism should rightly be called Corporatism, as it is the merger of corporate and government power."
Benito Mussolini

<u>Taxes</u>

"The power to tax is the power to destroy."
John Marshall

The average Colonial American paid a total tax rate between 5-7% to Britain before the war. After the Revolution, the average American paid a total tax rate between 1 and 1.5% in taxes. Today we pay on average 1.11% in property taxes, on average 8.9% in state taxes, and on average 15.3% in payroll taxes split in half between you and your employer. If you're self-employed—as a sole proprietor or business owner—you are responsible for the full amount. Additionally, 10 to 37% in federal taxes. And just to kick you while you're down, you must pay on average 5.1% sales tax on everything you already cannot afford. Not to mention the financial impact of tariffs and excise taxes.

So how much of your money do you have left for you and your family to survive on? But keep working yourself to death because our political elites are generous with your money. Giving 1.215 trillion dollars per year to welfare, one hundred billion plus to Ukraine, trillions to other countries, trillions to aid failing leftist states and cities. trillions to expand our ever-expanding bureaucracy. Trillions to wars you don't support, trillions of dollars' worth of military equipment given to terrorists our finest service members bled and died to protect us from and the list goes on and on and on. And don't forget about our national debt that has grown exponentially in the past decade and is now 34 trillion dollars. Meanwhile you struggle to put food on the table for your family. Ask yourself; is this what self-rule looks like?

When informed of her starving citizens not having any bread to eat; Marie Antoinette Queen of France replied, "Let them eat cake." The same soulless mocking mentality is now seen today by most of our own government leaders and representatives. Corruption will always exist in this world, as people by nature are corrupt. We can't rid ourselves of corruption, but a self-ruled society can change corruption's form and size to give the people and the individual more power over the corrupt. Maybe we can start by giving the people more power over their own money. While legislators require enough financial power to enforce their legislation, they have little restraints on how much financial power they have. So how much should they have? Or maybe the question should be how much financial power should we the people have? Could the citizens directly determine where at least a percentage of their tax dollars go? What if the people decide if or how much of their money goes overseas? Could individuals allocate percentages of their required taxes to departments and programs of their choosing? How much power can be taken away from the government and given to the people?

"I predict future happiness for Americans if they can prevent the government from wasting the labors of the people under the pretense of taking care of them."
Thomas Jefferson

Chapter 3
PRIVATIZATION

"Government even in its best state is but a necessary evil; in its worst state an intolerable one."

Thomas Paine

Power is essentially what all forms of government are all about. Power over people. So, a true political spectrum would be less about cultural issues and purely about power. With the governed on one side of the spectrum and the government on the other. With this we can easily see Socialism, Fascism, Communism, Monarchies, and Oligarchies all fall on the left side of the power spectrum and a Constitutional Republic on the right. The power spectrum is simply the individual minded vs the collective minded. Its, our resources, our objectives, our idea of morality, our destiny, vs my resources, my objectives, my idea of morality, my destiny. The collective views the individual as ignorant and selfish, the individual views the collective as a brainwashed cult of people unable to think for themselves. Every decade leftists try to revive and reinvent the same old failed and disturbed ideas of collectivism.

Government is a power-hungry monster that needs to constantly consume more and more power to sustain itself. This, with the fact that people are always trying to have more power than those around them, leads to governments always leaning left. No doubt our nation is farther left leaning towards a big, centralized government than it started out. History reveals what leaning left on the power spectrum leads to, but we have only gotten a taste of what leaning right can lead to. What does it look like when the government has as little power as practically possible? Can modern technology or new techniques replace the implementation of government power in certain ways?

In ancient times the basic need for organizing, controlling and regulating a society came from the natural chaos and injustice that comes about from large gatherings of people. So, people created governments to solve these basic problems. But this created positions of power. And power attracts the corrupt and power hungry like Flies to filth. Corruption of leaders and the dependency of their people leads to an increase in the size of government. More responsibilities equal more power and more government tasked with handling more responsibilities. Creating a natural power and bureaucracy snow balling effect. Best expressed by Oscar Wilde when he said, "The bureaucracy is expanding to meet the needs of the expanding bureaucracy." The federal government is the largest employer in the nation. With six times the number of employees as the top private sector employer and employs roughly six percent of the nation's population.

Government is an operational and efficiency nightmare. The irony is that bureaucracy was created with the intent of making government more efficient. But obviously more government doesn't make government more efficient. That's the equivalent of trying to fight fire with fire. We have all had the displeasure of interacting with government dysfunction in some form or another. The committees, agencies, departments and commissions, all dysfunctional, chaotic and only make things harder and more complicated. To top it off you get to pay for it with your tax dollars.

What if you could not only protest poor government but boycott it? Money is power, and if the government couldn't force you to give up your hard-earned money for everything, they want to spend your money on, then you the people would have more power, and the government would have less. I'm speaking of the concept known as Privatization. A process in which government agencies and services are transferred to private companies and contractors. Through Privatization one can "vote" with every dollar they spend.

Government is horribly inefficient, expensive and overbearing with power overreach. The best solution is to privatize nearly everything. A societal evolution toward less need for government. This would lead us as close to the long dreamed of concept of self-rule as possible. As in we rule ourselves and are not ruled over by big government. Private companies are without a doubt faster, cheaper, more efficient and have higher quality standards. Because private companies are financially incentivized to be more efficient, they are therefore incentivized to invest in technology to become ever more efficient.

Privatization is not a new concept, but one that societies have never truly committed to. History has countless examples of Privatization such as mercenaries, privateers and construction contractors. Today there are many forms already in use. Military contractors, construction contractors, private police, corrections, utilities, waste management, parks and park services, and more. We have it because it works and works better than the government. Privatization would provide a major economic boost, provide an abundance of jobs, create business opportunities, and make government overreach a thing of the past. Companies would compete with each other to do the best job for the lowest price. This is exactly what we are all already used to seeing work very well in our economy. The private sector actually requires results. Private companies and their workers with more freedom over their work and greater accountability, respond well to incentives as well, whereas government agencies and workers have little to no incentivized motivation and accountability. There is also the argument for legal issues. Say your child is injured on faulty playground equipment at a city or state park. Good luck winning a trial where the government has deeper pockets than you and no one holding them accountable. Whereas a small private company would be less financially formidable, and in most related scenarios, would also be held accountable to the community or the local government that hired them.

Any government service can be privatized to some degree. There are different forms and different levels of Privatization. A different level for each level of government and a different form for the allowed division of duties between the private company and the government agency. The government's role and power over these private companies would vary depending on these different levels, forms, importance, and security risks. The goal would be to privatize as much of our governments as possible within reason. In some cases, governments would have much control over these companies and in other cases less control. In some cases, governments would team up with companies, either working together or competing to give you the best and fastest service possible. In other cases, companies could completely replace government services. In the case of government services being completely replaced, citizens would have as much power over them as any other company if not more. In all cases instead of an agency or a politician doing a poor job and being allowed to continue, a company doing a poor job would be fired, voted out, boycotted or you as an individual would choose not to buy their product or service. Giving the average citizen more power, better more efficient service and allowing them to keep more of their hard-earned money. Privatization has the ability to create true checks and balances as well as unleash the full power of incentives that is so necessary to the success of a free society.

"We have it in our power to begin the world over again."

Thomas Paine

Chapter 4
THE GREAT EXPERIMENT

"The establishment of our new Government seemed to be the last great experiment for promoting human happiness."

George Washington

Amendment 10 States' rights- The powers not delegated to the United States by the Constitution, nor prohibited by it to the States, are reserved to the States respectively, or to the people.

The United States from its beginning has been a great experiment of self-rule and a Constitutional Republic. Self-rule can allow us as the human species to accomplish far more than we could even dream of. All we have to do is maintain and preserve it. What if humanity could freely experiment with different political, cultural, social, and economic concepts to scientifically pinpoint the best ideas to cultivate the future of human society?

This was generally the idea behind the formation of the states. Each state having its own government allowed for each state to rule itself and experiment with different ideas. Good ideas would lead to prosperity, and bad ideas would lead to a state's complete failure. People would leave the bad states and flock to the good ones. Sounds simple enough, and a great way to experiment while maintaining the security of the nation. Bad states should be allowed to fail, so long as their bad ideas and failures don't greatly harm the rest of the nation.

The only problem is when States are not allowed to fail or have their prosperity limited by federal government intervention. As stated in the 10th Amendment, government power and influence, was originally intended to be shaped like a pyramid with the smallest local forms of government having most influence over its people and the federal government having the least influence over people. Giving the most powerful levels of government the least amount of influence and the least powerful form of government the most influence. This was intended to ensure a government would be less able to oppress the governed. But the federal government is constantly giving a financial crutch to failing cities and states. Namely, leftist run cities and states. So, the prosperity of rightwing cities, states and taxpayers are being used to prop up failing leftist policies and ideas. The worst part is, because of this, leftists are actually convinced that their idiotic strategies are working. We need to show our citizens and the rest of humanity that leftist ideas are as embarrassingly absurd as they sound. At the same time, the federal government and its agencies are not allowing bad ideas to fail, they have now grown so big and powerful that its laws and regulations are crushing the potential prosperity of rightwing cities and states.

<u>Technology</u>

The federal government will also weaponize its agencies against freedom and prosperity through laws and regulations under the guise of public safety, bettering society, "saving the planet," "promoting energy efficiency" or "fighting racism." This is known as the Administrative State, or the unelected writing legislation and circumventing congress making this nation unrecognizable. One of the greatest and latest examples is the Environmental Protection Agency. As usual a government agency created with a seemingly noble cause, eventually transformed into a weapon of tyranny. Famous for its business and job killing regulations, it can now dictate which technologies Americans are allowed to use. The EPA is outlawing technologies such as gasoline and diesel engine propelled automobiles with no intent on stopping there. Next up we are likely to see its use banded on boats, aircraft, semi-trucks, yard equipment, farm equipment and recreational vehicles. This will create a financial strain on individuals and businesses as well as a strain on the economy and power grid. The short distance of EVs will also destroy the rural citizens' way of life. The leftist government is now on the war path to force us all to buy electric vehicles in order to save the planet from climate change without stopping to consider whether or not it actually is better for the environment. Let alone if they are practical or even what people want. EVs put far more carbon into the air than internal combustion engine vehicles. The manufacturing of these vehicles still generates carbon. The electricity they use is mostly created by burning coal, their batteries need to be replaced and recycled, minerals for their batteries must be mined, and the mines become depleted. All of this for what? Wildfires alone each year counteract any possible progress of limiting carbon emissions generated by vehicles. Not to mention how little of an effect human carbon emissions actually have on the planet. While we would lose our internal combustion engine economy, the rest of the world would gain it. Someday all ICE vehicles may be imported from other countries. Further hurting our economy and auto manufacturers.

Strict emissions standards have killed other technologies from even having the chance to develop and improve. Technologies such as the Wankel rotary engine and other Internal combustion engine technology. We need to give new technologies a break with restrictions and regulations in order for them to reach their full potential. They just may develop to surpass EPA standards and allow for greater efficiencies. But instead, the government would rather kill technologies and destroy the innovators that would have a potential to greatly impact society. This environmental crusade must stop before it Destroys our nation. They have gone as far as to burden our nation's agriculture in some states through taxing methane produced from cattle flatulence. Such idiotic leftist ideas are making their way to the federal government where they would then be used to burden all the other states. Technological freedom is a major reason this nation flourished so quickly. We used to be the greatest innovators in the world, and businesses, individuals, and the economy flourished.

<u>Oil</u>

Leftist and the EPA have been after oil companies for a long time. If it's not the inefficient EV process, it's the inefficient ethanol process that the leftists in power wage a crusade for, to put oil to death. I won't defend the oil companies, but the product itself is without a doubt a vital resource for the human race. We have the potential to be oil independent and to allow states that have this vital resource to harvest it for our nation and allow their economies to flourish. But the federal government and the EPA would rather give your money to other nations for their oil and burden these states and therefore our nation by use of regulations, permits and other restrictions. Oil imports are contributing greatly to our national debt; and for what reason? We have vast amounts of oil across our nation waiting to be harvested. The United States has one of the largest deposits of oil shale in the world and has a large portion of the world's oil reserves. Fracking is a process that would harvest vast amounts of oil for our nation, but it has been restricted. A process that with time could develop technology that could be more environmentally friendly. Oil is also very efficiently utilized. There is a wide range of products that use petroleum byproducts with over six thousand products. It's used for making plastics and synthetic materials, waxes, lubricating oils, rubber and paint. It's not just used for fueling a vehicle but is used to make many of the parts of your vehicle as well as the asphalt and road oil your vehicle drives on. This makes oil one of the most efficient and cost-effective products in the world. Our economy would boom if only the federal government would unchain our states.

Immigration

Our states and primarily our border states are under siege from illegal border jumpers and are then forced to have their hands tied behind their backs due to federal inaction as well as the federal government dictating how the state governments can solve this problem in their own way. Border jumpers may very well outnumber American citizens in the future. At the very least a government capable of reason should control the rate of immigration to allow time for assimilation so not to drown our nation's culture and principles with another's. Areas of a country also need time to adjust and grow with a population influx so not to become overwhelmed. Most obviously local law enforcement cannot deal with the crime increases. Hospitals, schools, businesses, job markets, housing, and local food supplies all feel the strain as well. Border jumpers include criminals trying to escape law enforcement and prosecution in their own country. They also include child sex traffickers, cartel drug traffickers, murderers, rapists and child molesters as many nations see our open border as a great way to get rid of all their criminals. Most likely they also include terrorists and enemy spies that are free to enter unchecked. Unfortunately, leftists only portray illegal border jumpers as innocent asylum seekers who have their reasons for not entering legally. The border states, individuals and the whole country must suffer because of this. Our border states should not be abandoned by the rest of us in the fight to protect the whole nation. We should be seen as traitors for abandoning them.

Justice

Individual, and therefore, state economic prosperity, is also greatly affected by law and order or the lack thereof. As criminals are being given more rights than law abiding citizens all across our nation, the federal government refuses to defend the constitution. People in general like to be able to defend themselves, their families, their businesses, their property, their neighbors and communities. But what we've seen lately, is the federal government and leftist elite politicians, not only not defending the constitution and standing up for individuals rights, but rather defend criminals and criminal actions of protesters who's protests politically align with those politicians. Rioters, thieves, home intruders and more. We have all seen the criminal either get away with the crime or get a slap on the wrist. Meanwhile the victim or good citizen becomes the one on trial and under attack for "their handling of the situation."

If rioters jump onto a roadway and you hit them with your vehicle, if they attack your vehicle or threaten your life, if they block your emergency service routes, legally, they win you lose. If you try to defend yourself, your family, your property, your livelihood, your community, the criminals win, you lose. In some cities squatters have more rights than the actual owner of a property. If you try to do the right thing and stop a crime such as theft, they win, you lose. In some cities, believe it or not, the law will not prosecute a thief if the amount stolen is under a certain amount. If you try to stop a theft at your place of employment, you will most likely lose your job. A corrupt society leads to corrupt judges and juries, which leads to unfair bias and backwards rulings. Corrupt judges and juries become more corrupt with greater susceptibility to bribery, threats, and pressure from our society.

Leftist politicians go through great lengths of effort to defend evil or use our system to attack the good in this country. We want justice! Not some made up idea of justice, such as social justice, but real justice. An individual punished for their crimes with punishments equal to the crime. We want criminals of severe crimes to stay in prison for their full sentence and not be released early, and not be enabled to commit the same type of crime again. When criminals are in prison, we want them to be treated like criminals and not like guests at a resort on vacation!

The morality of our nation's judicial system has quickly devolved as well. The Civil War was fought over our national definition of morality. Slavery, the ownership and mistreatment of another human being. Over 600,000 men had to die for our nation to rid itself of such an evil. Yet in recent decades abortion (the genocidal act of *legally* mutilating and murdering the most innocent, fragile and precious of human life) has plagued our nation for generations without a single shot being fired. Our founders made it clear LIFE, Liberty and the pursuit of happiness for all individuals. Our Supreme Court had gone in the opposite direction when it came to preserving and protecting human life. Something the federal government should be doing isn't, and only recently allowed states to choose for themselves.

Amendment 9-The enumeration in the Constitution of certain rights shall not be construed to deny or disparage others retained by the people. Currently leftist states have construed the 14 Amendment in a power grab attack on their political rival in the 2024 election as they attempt to ban a political candidate from the ballot in an attempt to reject the voting rights of the people. This doesn't sound like America, but rather an authoritarian government. This is a sign of the times. Things will only get worse. Tyranny will only grow in this nation. This outrageous act of Colorado's and other states could easily spark a civil war, yet the federal government is slow to act.

Justice for slavery? Yet another trend of the left that is becoming a reality in most leftist cesspools is the idiotic and tyrannical idea of reparations. You can't ever get justice for something that involves two deceased parties. Even if you hate this country and your dirt poor you still have it far better than anyone born in most other countries, especially the nations of American slave origins. You may find your reparations by taking a walk-through Arlington cemetery. Reparations is the new slavery, and the ultimate form of racism and tyranny. The government would steal the wages from its citizens and do so based on skin color and give it to those of another skin color. This is the most hateful fascist idea humanity has seen in a very long time.

Self-ruled people are intended to frequently self-reflect, decide if they are who they want to be, and make necessary adjustments accordingly. If this trend continues, of backwards justice, and ignoring states' rights, the U.S. constitution, the principle of self-rule, we are sure to see a future of complete tyranny. Including laws against the ordinary citizen and not the criminal. Dictating what products and technology you can have. Dictating how you heat your home, cook your food, and how you transport yourself to work. Unchecked politicians handing over your tax dollars to their favorite companies and technologies. The people of the United States cannot continue to allow such an overbearing leftist government to control their states in pursuit of pure tyranny over them. Our great nation, our great states, and our great people, are all held back, weighed down, and drained of great potential by the revolting parasite of leftism. Ask yourself; is this what self-rule looks like?

"Men should not petition for rights, but take them."
Thomas Paine

Chapter 5
FAITH AND FAMILY

<u>Divinely Inspired Cause</u>

"Of all the dispositions and habits which lead to political prosperity, religion and morality are indispensable supports. In vain would that man claim tribute to patriotism who should labor to subvert these great pillars of human happiness - these firmest props of the duties of men and citizens.... reason and experience both forbid us to expect that national morality can prevail in exclusion of religious principles."

George Washington

Freedom and liberty are extremely delicate due to human nature. They can be the worst of things when in the hands of the worst of people. Benjamin Franklin realized this threat to our nation when he warned us by stating, "Only a virtuous people are capable of freedom. As nations become corrupt and vicious, they have more need of masters." As well as John Adams When he stated, "Our Constitution was made only for a moral and religious people It is wholly inadequate to the government of any other."

Religion may have played a key role in creating a mindset leading to the ideas of individual freedom and self-rule. Concepts best expressed by Benjamin Franklin when he stated, "Freedom is not a gift bestowed upon us by other men, but a right that belongs to us by the laws of God and nature." and in the Declaration of Independence, "When in the Course of human events, it becomes necessary for one people to dissolve the political bands which have connected them with another, and to assume among the powers of the earth, the separate and equal station to which the Laws of Nature and of Nature's God entitle them, a decent respect to the opinions of mankind requires that they should declare the causes which impel them to the separation.

We hold these truths to be self-evident, that all men are created equal, that they are endowed by their Creator with certain unalienable Rights, that among these are Life, Liberty and the pursuit of Happiness.—That to secure these rights, Governments are instituted among Men, deriving their just powers from the consent of the governed, That whenever any Form of Government becomes destructive of these ends, it is the Right of the People to alter or to abolish it, and to institute new Government, laying its foundation on such principles and organizing its powers in such form, as to them shall seem most likely to affect their Safety and Happiness."

"Because power corrupts, society's demands for moral authority and character increase as the importance of the position increases."

John Adams

Because of religions' inspiring influence on individual freedom and self-rule, religion has always been a primary target for the power hungry. They can't have you thinking there is a higher power than them. They must have you see them as your god or as your ultimate authority. Making you the most obedient and humble servant they want and need you to be. Also, seeing the world through God's eyes allows you to see all that is wrong with the world. While those who see the world through their own eyes or allow themselves to be distracted, blindfolded, or led by others, will find it hard to see anything wrong with a world that revolves around them and feeds their desires. Therefore, the religious can never be content in this world, and the non-religious find it all too easy to be content. Contentment breeds complacency, and a complacent population is necessary for unlimited power grabs.

"Men must be governed by God, or they will be ruled by tyrants."

William Penn

<u>Families' vs The Self-Serving</u>

In this life, it can sometimes seem as if it's the world vs you and your family. You're trying to balance your ambitions with taking care of your family because family is more important than anything else in this world to you. Meanwhile, self-serving people often never build families because they are more interested in gaining money and power. This leads to them having the upper hand in society, allowing them to oppress you in many ways, while you are disadvantaged and trying to protect and provide for your family. A natural societal division created by differences in priorities, character and values. The things you'll most likely be thinking about when you're dying, are the things you should be focused on while you're living. Faith and Family first.

Character and values continue to naturally divide us by how we structure our families and raise our children. We are all responsible for the preservation of freedom in this country. But how do we preserve it? Freedom requires us to value and understand it. To have a respectful and courteous use of freedom, and to be courteous and respectful of others. My rights end where your rights begin. Some families, however, raise their children without an understanding or value of freedom. They raise them to abuse their freedom, and to be disrespectful and inconsiderate of others. They are lacking the characteristics of an adult and pass their childish mindsets on to their children who never seem to become adults. They see their rights and freedoms as more important than others. They are also raised to see society as the problem that needs to change instead of seeing themselves as needing improvement and growth. This creates a culture that starts to despise freedom because they despise what people do with freedom. They see less potential in freedom and more potential in big powerful government to keep those in check they wish to see kept in check with little consideration of a scenario in which the tables are turned or even a scenario in which their own side gains too much momentum and becomes extreme.

These people are often pro-majority rule democracy. The most popular and stealthy form of oppression. This way of thinking leads to not trusting anyone with freedom or even independence. They need conformity for easy control. But parents of their opposition keep raising their children with a different set of beliefs, morals, and values. So, they need to "raise" your children for you; or more accurately, brainwash them. Critical Race Theory and Diversity Equity and Inclusion are not the first and won't be the last of our so-called education systems' attempt at "politically guiding" our young people. They start the brainwashing process early and it continues through college. During my time in college, I attended a class in which the leftist professor asked the class, "who here is brave enough to admit they are a republican?" She might as well have asked, who is dumb enough? As I and the two others who raised our hands immediately realized things were going to be a lot more difficult for us in times to come. Our universities have perfected not only indoctrination, but discrimination. A stealthy filtering out process ensures only like-minded people graduate to get the jobs of influence and societal advantage. Thus, perpetuating the indoctrination in our school system. Homeschooling, possibly charter schools, may be our last resort but is not practical for most families. Especially financially. You still pay taxes for public schools even if your children are not attending.

The left seems to worship their own education in this country. Often used as a way to feel superior or used to dismiss their opponent's argument. But they don't seem to be teaching much of anything as they focus on indoctrination. Our cultural decay combined with our failing education system is creating the perfect storm for producing ignorant generations. Generations that don't care to learn from the past or from their opponents' arguments. Knowledge is useless without understanding, understanding is useless without application, and application is useless without wisdom.

Weak fathers and weak mothers create weak children. It's not just the parents that use "digital parenting" as in sticking their children in front of a screen so they won't have to actually be a parent, and it's not just the parents that can't look up from their phones to interact with their children. Fathers in many families are absent due to either a self-serving character or are either pushed away politically or culturally. Culturally pushed out of their children's lives as our anti-male culture discourages a strong father figure in the family and overly supports the nurturing role of the mother. This creates weak, needy, whiny, dependent minded children with a lack of respect for men and authority. Politically fathers are pushed out of families as our nation's welfare system continues to financially incentivize single motherhood. Men also have a natural desire to protect their families, but the left continues to create threats to your family and then they want to take away your ability to defend them physically and legally.

We need a culture that is not hostile towards men and encourages a man's natural desire to serve, provide and protect his family instead of a culture that encourages men to be self-serving. We need a government that at least doesn't incentivize the destruction of the family, but rather incentivizes the creation of the family. We need a government that invests in adoption services more than it invests in abortion services.

We have created a society of weak men and women. Between their leftist parents and their leftist teachers from elementary through college, leftist children never stand a chance to learn how to think for themselves, become decent people or even become adults. Then they enter society where they vote and try to destroy society in every way possible. They vote on societal issues they themselves are not invested in. They are often not homeowners, they often do not have children, they often have not even worked in the work force as they have only gone to college and have had their parents take care of them. Yet they continue to vote on things they do not understand or have any stake in.

These leftist children have often been brainwashed into having a hatred for Christianity as it is the opposite of a self-serving lifestyle that they seem to worship as their very own religion. Amoral, indecent parents of an amoral, indecent society raise amoral, indecent children. We have all seen what these incoming generations of leftist children are doing to our society. From something as small as their terrible manners, demeanor and customer service, to over sexualization, to mass shootings.

Our children are under attack from the left in this culture war. School libraries have pornographic material in them, the classrooms have more rainbow cult flags than American flags, drag queens are on children's television shows, drag shows are out in public, inappropriate pride parades are out in public, children's books indoctrinate our children with stories of leftist politicians, gay rights, anti-America slave stories, black pride and race focused stories. Teachers are brainwashing our children, and school shootings are on the rise. Some states are even allowing the satanic temple to have an "after school Satan club" for kids. If our children's emotional, mental and spiritual well-being isn't being threatened, it's their physical well-being. We can't afford to continue to send our children to the front lines of this culture/cold war while we, decade after decade continue to hope "it's just a phase this country is going through" or think, "I as a parent can counter the brainwashing." I wonder what kind of nation we will be leaving to our children if we continue to pretend as if our union with leftists isn't destroying our society.

"If there must be trouble, let it be in my days, that my child may have peace."

Thomas Paine

<u>God or No God</u>

Religion or lack of religion can also create differences in character and values to form perhaps the greatest of all cultural divisions. Right and wrong, what's acceptable, what's not acceptable, perceptions of reality, value of life, understanding of freedom, and liberty. The right answers are revealed by asking the right questions.

Social and cultural divisions form from naturally evolving differences. The greatest of these is the God or no God decision. Every societal, cultural, moral and political argument in the history of the human race, can trace its roots back to this God or no God decision that each individual makes for themselves. This question branches off into seemingly infinite questions. Is there absolute truth or is truth subjective? Is morality objective or subjective? Is life about me or about God? Do I serve myself or do I serve God? Should humans' rule over each other or is God the ultimate authority over humanity? Do we give value to each other or is value given to each individual by God? Does life have meaning or is it meaningless? Does my life have purpose or not? Does free will exist? Does God love us? And the list goes on. These questions answered, direct our lives in one of two directions. One life has hope, and the other does not.

Whether it's about abortion, government, LGBT+ movement, the death penalty, academic curriculum, taxes, the economy, or war, our stance on all issues is determined by our answer to the foundational question. God or no God?

Morality and Protecting the Innocent

Morality is among the greatest dividing factors in every society. Without morality a society rapidly decays and descends into chaos. From denying God to denying science to denying reality, and all logic and reason. Like a child they seek out only their emotional wants and none that seem to even be in their own best interest or for their betterment.

"Religion and good morals are the only solid foundation of public liberty and happiness."

Samuel Adams

The left have managed to pervert and corrupt everything in our society not just science. There is no greater victim of a lack of morality than the innocent. The innocent have always been a target for the wicked. They now believe in "chest feeding," one of the most disgusting and disturbing of all hideous leftist heathen beliefs. What else would we expect from a nation that turned from God into the hands of evils perversions? Precious innocent babies are being preyed upon and devoured by the wicked every day in this world as we stand by and do nothing out of fear of being "too extreme." The satanic temple cult is now being recognized as a national religion, giving it religious freedom rights, which are then used to circumvent state abortion laws as it claims abortion is part of its religion in its satanic abortion ritual practices. Maybe we should start an anti-leftist law, culture, and authority religion in opposition of theirs. The leftists have completely reversed our nation's morality of innocent life. They have a disgusting compassion for pedophiles, while they torture and murder unborn babies. It used to be, kill the wicked and defend the innocent with your life. Now it's, kill the innocent and defend the wicked. The left has infiltrated our justice system and culture. They love to defend the wicked. How much more must we watch of pedophiles, rapists, murders, serial killers getting a slap on the wrist for their wicked atrocious crimes against the innocent and humanity. It should be an eye for an eye. You forfeit your right to live when you deny someone else their right to live. On Gods authority we may put an end to the life of someone so wicked. The punishment must fit the crime. Anything less than a prompt execution for these predators is absurd. If these wicked demons wish to bring hell to the innocent, the least we can do is make it our duty to send them to the hell they so desire.

Just as we have rights given to us by God and not by man, human beings have *value* that is not given to them by man, but by God their creator. If human beings did have such authority, I'd ask which life is more of value? The pure, innocent and delicate life in the woman's womb? Or the woman willing to torture and kill that beautiful life? That life belongs to its creator, not you. God creates beauty, and evil seeks to destroy it. To deny a person their God given value is to wage war against God himself.

We fought a civil war in defense of human life and value once before, is the cause of the innocent any less of a cause? If we believe God gives us a soul at conception, then why aren't we fighting to protect that soul? What are we waiting for? This is not a cause for debate over legality, this is a cause for war and nothing less. If the same God who said, "there is a time for war," shows you a wicked enemy that preys on everything that is a reflection of him, also gives you the strength and capability to do something about it, shouldn't you? Shouldn't the good in this world fight back against evils aggression with just as much aggression if not more? We need to do more than shrug our shoulders and tell ourselves we tried. Let what pains God, pain us, and let us be God's tools for justice.

Culture

The opposition will continue its dehumanization of babies and children campaign until they are of less value to them than their material possessions. We've seen this in the latest leftwing agendas that accept murder up until birth. They even push for after birth murder. Planned Parenthood was even caught in the disgusting act of selling body parts on the black market, which I might add, never resulted in the government ceasing to fund it. Even commercials attempting to stop people from accidentally killing their babies by forgetting them in their hot cars, remind people to "try putting something of value in the back seat, like a purse," so you can see you have a child back there. We continue to perpetuate dehumanization in our culture by allowing this to be the current cultural norm. Incoming generations will not think twice of such cultural norms. And evil concepts have a way of growing beyond our control over time. "A long habit of not thinking a thing wrong gives it a superficial appearance of being right." Thomas Paine. Dehumanization is the worst of diseases on this planet. It leads to the worst of ideas. Eugenics, genocide, abortion, rape, slavery, racism, child abuse, child sex abuse, domestic abuse, elder abuse, murder, etc. It is the ultimate form of a self-centered mindset. Elevating your own value while lowering someone else's.

Heathenism leads to an oppressive society through the creation of hierarchies as a "me centered" society becomes the replacement alternative to a God centered society. This then quickly leads to a subjective take on morality which is then used in the form of "social justice" to be a tool to elevate some and oppress others. There is little contrast between ancient heathens and modern-day heathens. They used to worship nature, and still do by way of environmental activism and the climate change movement. It requires great faith to believe in climate change to the extent they do, yet they let it dictate their entire lives and the functionality of their nations and the entire human race. They used to perform infant human sacrifices, and still do by way of abortion. Sacrificing their own child to their new god; themselves. Heathens used to proclaim their leaders and governments as divine; and they still do by allowing a complete submission of their freedoms and way of life.

With no God to give them or their lives value, people start to try and find ways to elevate themselves and devalue others. Devaluing human life leads to the elevating of another life, leading to emperors, kings, dictators who all have treated others like cattle or worse. But a Christian perspective leads to the belief that all men are created equal, our rights come from God not man, we can rule ourselves. Emperors of ancient Egypt, China, Rome, Incan and Aztec empires all saw themselves as God's. Ancient Greek, Persian and many other emperors thought of themselves as equal to their gods or demigods, or at least believed their gods favored them. A way to justify their rule over others. A mighty empire forged in conquest and hierarchy would glorify the emperor through the size and power of the empire, and through elevating oneself above others by sacrificing people in conquest or enslaving them to build great works.

While all other religions are designed to serve man through worldly things, Christianity has man giving up worldly things in exchange for a relationship with God. This directly influenced the foundational principles of the United States, as all other nations were designed with the people serving their governments and worldly leaders' narcissism, instead we made the leaders and all people equals under God.

Separation of church and state doesn't mean keeping religious people or religion out of our government as some on the left would love to see. It means don't let the church rule over the state and don't let the state rule over the church. In this, no religion could ever rule over another. At least directly. But indirectly it does, always has and always will happen. If it's a belief, it's a religion, and the anti-God religion has taken over the state and is ruling over the other religions.

The self-proclaimed party of "science" is weaponizing science through political means. They use religious and political bias when examining and interpreting data. They use it to dismiss their oppositions arguments and beliefs by labeling it as a "religious belief" and therefore is not based on "science" and therefore not a logical argument to be taken seriously. The left claims to be the party of science, though they don't seem to know what a chromosome is, they think our emotions trump reality, they think a man can breastfeed a baby, they think a fetus is the mothers body, they think a fetus with all the proper DNA isn't human and dismiss the argument to be "religious", they claim billions of years of heterosexual reproductive evolution suddenly led to homosexuality. They believe in the beginning there was nothing, and nothing exploded for no reason to create everything. And a puddle of mud getting struck by lightning created all life on earth. But to them, to believe in God is a crazy stretch. One can believe in God and still acknowledge life's natural processes for what they are. A belief in God appears to actually make it easier to study natural processes, based off of what has been observed of the heathen lefts inabilities to perform actual and unbiased scientific research. During Covid we saw Christians tend to favor natural immunity, vitamins, and medicine while the left favored an untested mystery vaccine. They thought a basic mask and six feet of distance could stop a virus from spreading. Then when called on their faulty "science" they tripled their masks and booster shots. The data is now out and to no surprise they were wrong about almost everything.

The secular world view keeps them from acknowledging sin and evil allowing everything, including views of truth, decency, and morality to be twisted, contorted, and perverted in any and every way. They have zero contrast between right and wrong. Things such as love and justice have no definition, so they are given one by the individual. The truth of what human beings are and why they exist is lost or tainted. What is influenced by sin and evil and is unnatural, confuses them and is passed off as being either "natural" for human beings, or if unacceptable to the culture it is passed off as a mental health issue.

Sin may at times feel natural as we are naturally drawn towards it, but once in its presence we realize it is anything but natural. We realize in order to stay in the presence of sin we must turn from what is natural and surrender our humanity. The more someone of reason tries to use science to excuse their sin and warped view of reality, the more they realize science and reason cannot, and instead points them in the opposite direction. Towards God and Christianity. Heathen empires never last as society becomes dysfunctional from the decay of a valueless sin centered culture.

When you seek the truth instead of yourself, you tend to find it.

In many ways Leftism has proven to be Satanism in a not so clever disguise including body mutilation, murder of babies, and perversion of sex. We are under attack, the worlds on fire under the control of evil, the innocent are murdered and tortured, predators roam free, and yet God's soldiers stand idly by and hide; "waiting for his direction". God won't steer a vehicle that isn't in motion. We already have the knowledge and wisdom of Gods sovereign guidance. Throughout the Bible; God has made it *very* clear, he does not like wicked cultures spreading their influence from one generation to the next. Human beings may have traded God for sin in the beginning; but this world is still under Gods authority, and as Christians, it is our soldier's duty to enforce his authority and guard all that is his. It's time for Christians to start flipping tables. As our culture seems to resemble Sodom and

Gomorrah, perhaps it's even time for a fire and brimstone approach.

Anti-Christian

The religious and non-religious find each other unbearable. The religious have managed to live with the non-religious, but the non-religious seem to wish to completely annihilate religion all together. There has always been extreme aggression towards Christians and Christian culture, but this aggression in this country seems to be getting exponentially worse and conflicts more frequent. From physical attacks, including mass shootings in churches and Christian schools, to legal attacks on churches, the right to assemble, and on Christian protesters. Anti-Semitism has also increased rapidly and aggressively. There has also been a not so hidden war on the Bible as countless attempts to disprove it have been made. Attempts that viciously attack every story in the Bible, and even go as far as to completely deny any historical information the Bible has to offer. They do this for the sole purpose of attacking Christianity and in no way in pursuit of the truth. They will gladly erase history if it helps to erase the Bible. They are even constantly spreading lies about the crusades in hopes to rewrite history to portray Christians as villainous as possible.

Most detestable of attacks on Christian culture has been the relentless assault on Christian holiday celebrations. Our Saviors birth and resurrection have both been turned into pagan holidays to worship magic, fairy tale myths, materialism and consumerism. Things are only getting rapidly worse. Banks had started closing accounts of Christian organizations with no explanation as to why. Government healthcare insurance pays for abortions and transitional surgeries using Christian tax dollars to pay for them. In 2024 Easter Sunday was proclaimed by the president of the United States and many local governments to be "transgender day." Additionally, and perhaps most unsettling, Science and conformity have always been at odds with one another (and rightfully so), but now they are aggressively and disturbingly teamed up. You are no longer allowed to question, research, or think for yourself.

Today calling yourself a Christian puts a target on your back. Leftists immediately label you as the reason for all of their problems as they see you as their religious and political enemy. Maybe it's time we except this label. They would deny the truth if their political opposition was tied to it. They will always attempt to discourage or attack any form of moral guidance or opinion. Christians always have been and always will be hated for opposing sin and much of what secularists consider to be "natural" or "their right to choose."

Justice

Our founders set up our nation to make it easier for a people to resolve an injustice done to them by their government. The injustices the left tries to resolve today, are not injustices of government or society, but rather injustices of a sinful human nature. The heathen left predictably created what they call "social justice." A ridiculous yet scary idea of justice in which the mob decides what is just. How else would a world without God carry out justice? More often than not, it will be for revenge or playing the blame game and be fueled by their struggle for purpose and justice in a world without either and can only be found through God.

If there was a perfect form of government, it would never involve a king. But if it were possible for a king to be truly wise, truly unbiasedly just, and truly pure and good to have only the best interest in mind for the people, then no one should hesitate to bend a knee to such a perfect King. But this world is lost to find such a King, and so humanity is cursed with never-ending warfare, and we are left not with the question; do we fight or not, but rather do we fight for man or for freedom.

War

Warfare is a byproduct of sin, so mankind will always be at war with itself. Since Cain killed Able humanity has permitted and evil has promoted, the slaughtering of God's children by the billions. Christians have no choice but to cower or stand up to the evil in this world as their duty requires. If warfare is to be the destiny of man, let us now decide what we fight and die for. An army of evil men requires an army of good men to face it. "The only thing necessary for the triumph of evil is for good men to do nothing." Edmund Burke

This division continues to grow wider and wider as our culture rejects the anchor of Christianity and dedicates its destiny to the direction of the wind. As our culture rejects God, it at minimum rejects the separation between human and animal. Our culture believes we evolved from animals and therefore are animals. So how long before people who believe they are animals begin to act like it? A perverse perspective on reality leads to an even more perverse reality. From people who see themselves above all others, to people who believe morality is determined by the consensus, or people who believe morality is relative, to people who let their emotions and hormones guide their decisions, to people who think they can choose their gender, age, or even species by believing reality itself is relative. The result branches off of this God or no God belief and has fueled the political divide and with many cultural issues, has actually been the catalyst of the political division. By now I don't think it's a secret to anyone that most Christians and religious people find themselves on the right side of the isle while most atheists and heathens find themselves on the left side. This division in the human race has existed as long as humans have but has been dealt with on a national level. But as human society evolves and communication technology unites ideas on a global level, we are and will see the God or no God divide on a global scale. Perhaps resulting in a global conflict, possibly resulting in the elimination of believers.

Christians and Jews have been hunted, imprisoned, enslaved, tortured, and executed since the beginning. Almost as if some dark force has a hold of humanity and directs hatred towards Christians and Jews. The ancient people, Egyptians, Romans, Islamic empires, Kings, Fascists, and Communists all tried their hardest to persecute Christians and Jews to the greatest of their abilities. So, we fled to the new world the first chance we had. Oppression followed us over here. After building the greatest nation the world has ever seen, faster than the world has ever seen, we are now once more facing hostility, outnumbered and up against a wall. They will find new ways to stone us for standing up for our beliefs, and they will find new ways to burn us alive for not bending a knee to their idols. Fight or flight? With the option of flight now removed, the choice is obvious.

As our nation's culture decays, our troubles will only increase as we continue to attempt to maintain this unequally yoked relationship. As this continents first settlers knew, religion cannot remain uninjured in oppressive lands. What should the religious do when there is nowhere else to flee to? We cannot run from the wicked or oppressive forever. Separation is necessary, if not for self-rule, then to save the faith from corruption and oppression. The oppressors can choose if by peaceful means or not. If any man is best prepared to sacrifice it all, that man would without a doubt be a Christian man with all of eternity secured. Oppressive attacks on Christians and other religions continue to escalate. The attacks on our family first culture, attacks on our children, attacks on the innocent, attacks on our Christian influenced nation's founding principles. The division grows as the branches of the God or no God foundational belief branch out as far as our culture will take it. Would my fellow Christians say this nation is currently friendly towards them or hostile? Are Christians capable of self-rule in this country? Or are we constantly oppressed by federal and local governments as well as our nation's culture? Would they say this nation is currently fertile ground for cultivating a nation that serves God or at least doesn't oppose God? Our culture now spits in God's face. What was once an asylum for Christians has now become either our prison or last stand.

Chapter 6
FREEDOM

"The best way to take control over a people and control them utterly is to take a little of their freedom at a time, to erode rights by a thousand tiny and almost imperceptible reductions. In this way, the people will not see those rights and freedoms being removed until past the point at which these changes cannot be reversed."

Pat Miller

We human beings have been fighting the same power struggle war since the beginning of time. If happiness is able to be found in this life, freedom provides the environment necessary for it to grow. Freedom is what we live for. Freedom is what we fight for. And freedom is what we are willing to die for. It's getting harder and harder to see freedom when we look at the modern United States. We see crony capitalism, corruption, theft, injustice, and laws designed to take away freedoms rather than preserve them. What do we mean when we talk about freedom in this country? Leftists are often confused by the concept of freedom and what it means in this country, so I thought I would briefly attempt to clarify. Depending on the context, we could be talking about freedom as a people, as in the ability to self-rule and guide our own government, or we could be talking about individual freedom, as in the ability to remain free of oppression from other individuals as well as a government infringing on our personal rights and liberties. Unfortunately, most human beings barely understand concepts involving freedom when it's their own freedom at stake, let alone someone else's freedom at stake. We must work together to preserve each other's freedom and individual rights. If you're looking for those who are passionate about freedom, America is where you'll find them. They are called American Patriots.

Safety and Freedom

"The greatest tyrannies are always perpetrated in the name of the noblest causes."

Thomas Paine

The excuse of safety has more often than not been the primary reason for loss of freedom in every society. Benjamin Franklin said it best when he said, "Any society that will give up a little liberty to gain a little security will deserve neither and lose both." This must not be tolerated, as Thomas Jefferson stated, "There is no justification for taking away individuals' freedom in the guise of public safety." But where did this idea of safety over freedom come from? It developed through early human history and flourished up until the American Revolution. A great example of this is the time of landlords, kings and castles. The choice was simple, live in the wilderness and be free but vulnerable or live under a ruler on their lands with high taxes, no freedom but have the protection of an army and a castle. If you couldn't decide, the choice was made for you when all land eventually became owned by a ruler.

After generations, being ruled was a natural indoctrination of your reality. To this day those in the old world remain complacent and accepting of big government dominance over them, as they've never known anything else. From a seemingly necessary way to survive to a collective mindset of putting the desperate paranoid wants of the masses over the necessary freedoms of the individual.

With unclaimed land unavailable to provide freedom for people, those who valued freedom fled to the new world with other likeminded individuals from all over. This is one of the biggest reasons why the United States is one of the last strongholds of individual freedom in the world. But complacency is spreading, and freedom is disappearing. Like a frog being slowly boiled alive, we are unaware of our slow loss of freedom and the dangers of choosing safety over freedom repeatedly over time.

Liberty minded individuals are running out of places to escape to. When you're backed into a corner there is only one option left, stand and fight. And we just might have to sooner rather than later with the 2nd Amendment being a major victim and target of safety over freedom thinkers. As mass shootings are on the rise, the left blames the gun not the shooter, in an attempt to harness the power of the Stampeding panic of "sheeple" in order to achieve their goals of policy and power. When "sheeple" stampede we get trampled. Or how about environmentalism. How many times have they told us the world will end if we don't yield to their extreme environmental policies? Of which are all regulations, control, and more power to the federal government.

It's for your own good, it's for your own safety, said every government in history as they gained your compliance in handing over your freedoms. There's no greater example of this than the government's response to the outbreak of Covid19. Not only did we witness governments all over the world doing this, but we saw the governments of the world work together in an effort to restrain and oppress all of mankind. The leaders of the world's nations surrendered their responsibility of wisdom and discernment to their personally anointed leaders of the World Health Organization. In the U.S., the CDC and a certain "Dr." whose name I don't care to mention. If all the world's government elites would unite to oppress the people of the world, then perhaps the people of the world should unite to fight for freedom and throw off the oppression of our governments. An unfortunate impossibly as the "sheeple" of the world are always the most inconvenient hurdle of intelligent direction. Like sheep these people cannot think for themselves and always follow the idiot in front of them or listen to anyone who speaks loud enough. From the masks to the vaccines to the lock downs, there are just too many examples of them. Even intelligent people can become fools when panic sets in. The panic seems to be never-ending at this point. We cannot forget the lines that were crossed and the aggression between opposing sides. One side of those who were cautious, full of speculation, thought for themselves, valued freedom, saw the bigger picture of what was going on, and how vulnerable we were to an authoritarian take over and the other side of panic, short sightedness, gullible, followers, minions who told on their neighbors like it was Nazi Germany, and were willing to hand over the nation and their freedoms on a silver platter in order to avoid one of the least life threatening global pandemics the world has ever seen. Remember the abandoning of the Constitution, the abuse of authority, citizens becoming prisoners in their own homes, the destruction to our economy we will never recover from, the power they had over our employment, our income, our travel, our families, our bodies, our choice. Our loved ones that suffered and passed away in hospital care, did so all alone as we were not allowed to sit by their sides holding their hands and comforting them. We all just let oppression take over our lives as we held onto the belief that it was all going to end soon. But weeks turned into months and months turned into years. Do we really believe the power-hungry won't cease their golden opportunity the next time a pandemic hits? Do the most moderate among us really believe a civil war powder keg isn't waiting for the next pandemic? If we do not organize and prepare to defend our nation and its freedoms, do we really think this free nation will survive another round of this madness? Perhaps those involved in "the new world order" already have plans for such an orchestrated event.

Ask yourself; is this what self-rule looks like? When you oppress people, you create a storm that quickly grows beyond your control. A storm with resistance like thunder and rage like lightning. Today, a dark cloud looms over this nation once again.

"I hold it, that a little rebellion, now and then, is a good thing, and as necessary in the political world as storms in the physical."

Thomas Jefferson

<u>Freedom of Speech</u>

"Freedom had been hunted round the globe; reason was considered as rebellion; and the slavery of fear had made men afraid to think. But such is the irresistible nature of truth, that all it asks, and all it wants, is the liberty of appearing."

Thomas Paine

Amendment I- "Congress shall make no law respecting an establishment of religion or prohibiting the free exercise thereof; or abridging the freedom of speech, or of the press; or the right of the people peaceably to assemble, and to petition the government for a redress of grievances."

U.S. Constitution

Those who are truly oppressed are the ones who cannot say that they are oppressed without being silenced or mocked for saying so. Where power is to be had, it will be taken; where power is taken it will be abused. Freedom of speech is necessary for all other freedoms to exist and to fight oppression and wrongs in a peaceful way. This makes freedom of speech the foundation of a peaceful, happy, decent, virtuous, functional, capable and prosperous society. A society without the freedom of speech is a violent, angry, indecent, immoral, dysfunctional, incapable,

61

decaying society. Individuals are to a society as cells are to a body. If they can't communicate with each other this creates a lot of issues leading to bigger issues and the body begins to die.

During the Covid19 lock downs, in some places, it was essentially illegal to assemble. Making it illegal to protest against the government, and even illegal to go to church. The leftist media made any antigovernment protester out to be a terrorist. At the same time the leftist agenda protests were completely acceptable to them. Silencing the opposition is the easiest and often the first tactic used in the creation of a tyrannical government.

"If freedom of speech is taken away, then dumb and silent we may be led, like sheep to the slaughter."
George Washington.

Our society is quickly giving up freedom of speech. Everything and anything the opposition is angered by; they label it hate speech and even destroy objects of historical significance. Instead of engaging in civil dialog they have a temper tantrum. Instead of a peaceful protest they riot and loot. The powers that be can digitally censor us on social media platforms. We are so called, "fact checked" by those with agendas. They call their opinion fact and label the opinion of their opposition as false "misinformation." Tyranny doesn't appear everywhere at once, but it rather seeds itself in fertile soil and spreads like an aggressive weed. Some cities and even states have fallen into the early and rapid growth of tyranny where all opposition is silenced by the mob majority. If our voice is on a sign, the sign is graffitied. If our voice is on a building, the building is vandalized. If your voice is on your clothing, it is torn off your body. If your voice is a flag, it is burned.

Our nation is even becoming an upside-down world. Some label speech they don't like as violence, but speech that's harming to children as freedom of speech. If a pride flag is burned it's a hate crime, if you burn our national flag that stands for everything many have fought and died for, it's okay, it's just protesting. If you don't march in perfect lockstep with them, they label you a fascist. They hate you for your gender, your race, your sexual orientation, then call you a hateful sexist, racist, homophobe. Even our pledge of allegiance and our national anthem are under attack. This has gone too far, and we cannot undo what's been done.

Artistic Freedom

"He who dares not offend cannot be honest."
Thomas Paine

Artistic freedom has always been a popular way for people to express themselves, especially when feeling oppressed. What we've been seeing, is a "cancel culture" label any and every artistic expression, discussion and protest as "offensive" or "hate speech" in an attempt to silence their opposition. With completely absurd accusations they try their hardest to show in the most roundabout way possible how "it's connected to racism." And companies almost always give in to these lunatic loud mouths. Comedy is under attack, music is under attack, television is under attack, radio is under attack, and even movies are under attack. This is exactly what has been witnessed at the onset of Fascist and Communist takeovers within the last century. Soon we are likely to see a ban of books and even items of historical significance, when they become "to offensive" to the leftists.

"Freedom of speech is a principal pillar of a free government; when this support is taken away, the constitution of a free society is dissolved, and tyranny is erected on its ruins."

Benjamin Franklin

<u>Pandering, Propaganda and Indoctrination</u>

"If you tell a big enough lie and tell it frequently enough it will be believed."

Adolf Hitler

History has shown us that once the left silence their opposition, they waste no time making good use of all their obtained microphones. From culture war ammunition, to indoctrination, to just straight up propaganda.

The left's culture war tactics have been very obvious despite their attempts to be subtle. Their pandering started as the idea to equalize race representations in movies and television despite actual race proportions in society. It has since then evolved into an embarrassingly obnoxious campaign of pandering to minority groups and demographics by saturating entertainment and media with anyone who is *not* straight, white, conservative, Christian or male.

Every form of entertainment is controlled by the left. From standup comedy to television shows to every movie Hollywood has produced. Even children's cartoons are phasing out little white boys or characters. They go further in cartoons to have even started depicting gender neutral, drag queens and homosexual parent characters. When there is any kind of children's education, they at the very least, will try to avoid inspiring little white boys and will always primarily focus on inspiring girls. Odd considering the left doesn't acknowledge there only being two genders. But in doing so, they also are unknowingly doing girls a disservice by projecting their limited view of what success and accomplishments look like. What's more disturbing is that these inspirational accomplished female idols are only being acknowledged because they are women, when we should really be inspiring <u>all</u> children to develop <u>character</u> traits of <u>good</u> people that lead to them <u>doing good</u> and making a difference. Harriet Tubman for example, should be given recognition, not because she was a black woman, but a good person who had the necessary character to do the right thing when goodness was needed most.

This pandering indoctrination is without a doubt a hostile takeover of our culture in a desperate attempt to normalize their view of how our culture should be and villainize or erase what they hate about our current culture. The pandering continues as everything in the entertainment industry and especially in children's cartoons, is now all about social injustices of the past and race and gender "equality," AKA superiority. A never-ending waterboarding for the white man in their social justice crusade. It's as if the more they stomp on straight, white, Christian, men, the more they feel they are somehow adding value and meaning to their lives. Businesses have also joined the woke pandering cancel culture. We are seeing a continued rise of pandering woke commercials. All different types of businesses pandering to women, African Americans, homosexuals and transsexuals. We are even seeing people rewrite history by claiming that minorities have invented things they didn't or had actually just contributed to. The pathetic and sickening pandering of course doesn't stop there as it seems like every other day there is a new day, week, or month that is dedicated to recognition of minority groups as they drowned out recognition of those more deserving, such as veterans and first responders, in this never ending woke pandering parade.

Rewriting History

Information that enters the mind persuades the mind. Control the information that enters the mind, control what persuades the mind. When new information spreads so fast, historic information doesn't have a chance to enter the minds of the new generations. Lies are spreading faster than truth because truth must be verified and is only verified by truth seekers, falsehoods are emotionally accepted. In this acceptance no attempt is made to verify the information. When a people do not believe in objective truth, then belief in what information is true is guaranteed to be easily swayed in any direction by those in control of the spread of information. A rejection of objective truth is a rejection of intellect and reason, and a submission to emotional ignorance, guidance, and irrationality.

The truth is often very controversial to the left in many ways. Historical truth is one of these ways. As they sprint towards communism, they always make sure to establish the victims and villains in their target society. In order to control and indoctrinate, they need to control the narrative in their made-up stories and the premise of their questions. This can be seen in the way they depict history in their movies and television shows, and through teachings such as Critical Race Theory and their Diversity Equity and Inclusion indoctrination courses, as they never tire in their conquest to rewrite history as all oppressors always do. Rewriting and erasing history has been done by tyrants all over the world since the beginning of time as a way to keep the people ignorant. They do this at the very least by depicting history through the emotional filter of their own modern-day perspective and hindsight. Of which is also influenced by the little they actually know of history, and as portrayed, filtered, and exaggerated by their leftist professors. A secularist perspective of human history always leads to the blame game, instead of acknowledging that the evils and injustices that were done throughout history were a result of a sinful human nature being the root cause, and not the sole fault of a particular nation, culture, race, gender, sexual orientation, or religious belief. Furthermore, evils and injustices in history were done as a result of a culture of people not thinking it wrong as the cultures of the previous generations did even worse. Going back far enough we see most cultures committing to evil and unjust acts by justifying them as a way of survival. Living in the world's sole superpower or first world country for one's entire life in the modern day, is a perfect way to lose the ability to understand our ancestor's perspective, their circumstances, and desperation. All human beings are capable of anything so long as their circumstances provide the opportunity. This leads me to bring to your attention another way the left has been erasing and rewriting history. Our historical figures along with historical statues and structures have been under attack for a while. Everyone and everything are being labeled as racist, sexist, homophobic, and bigoted. New generations are taught to have zero understanding for history, let alone respect for it. It's because of our past generation's perspectives, and what happened in their time period, that we are allowed and able to have our perspectives in our time period.

Why does history matter? Because no matter the topic, the problem, the conflict; there is always a before. The before that explains how we got to this, and how do we move forward. Too often these days we examine either today's events as if they appeared out of thin air, or we see the actions of those from another time as though they should have known better. We also fail to acknowledge that for every event today, there is an after. We deserve nothing less than to be judged by those in the future as ignorantly as we have judged those before us.

Media and Leftist Commercials

The media is the most famous of all propaganda. Freedom of the press is yet another double-edged sword. When used correctly it can be the greatest weapon for freedom. But if used incorrectly it can become the greatest weapon against freedom. A good journalist has the power to inform the people of truths that have been hidden from them and to circumvent propaganda. This is extremely important and necessary for a free society. A bad journalist is a propagandist and is one who spreads either false information or information that is twisted to fit a political narrative or agenda. Both of which are fed to the bad journalist by a source with power over them. In this they make themselves servants of evil doers and destroyers of a free society.

It seems more often than not; the media has become the greatest weapon against freedom. Yet another symptom of a corrupt and decaying society. During Covid I witnessed very disturbing commercials that made me question whether or not I was actually watching a sci-fi movie about a Fascist tyrannical society. The commercial was created by a local news network and was just another obnoxious and forceful propaganda attempting to guilt people into getting the vaccine. One actor after the next said why they got the vaccine stating it was for their family members. Insinuating that if you don't get the vaccine, you were killing your loved ones. The media was saturated in disgusting and overly pushy propaganda like this. And that's the least of what people in more densely populated areas were experiencing. The media soon created an army of sheeple to attack anyone who didn't get the vaccine and label them as terrorists.

Commercials for political ads have also gone too far. Political ads have always been over the top but lately they've become more and more outrageous. They'll label their opponent as a racist or accuse them of sexual assault. The claims, lies, and accusations are nothing short of defamation and the media fans the flames. The worst of accusations always seem to be right before an election. Just in time to influence the outcome of the election without giving the opponent optimal time to refute the claims. The left has perfected this strategy.

When the media isn't manufacturing its own news stories, it's either a one-sided bias take on an event, or they put a spin on the story to make it about what they want it to be about for their political agendas. They know lies captivate an audience more than truth. We've all seen the abuse of editing audio or footage to use it for or against someone or something. They have Perfected defamation with rapid fire release. When we protest, they say it's an end to democracy. When they riot, they say it is the voice of the people. They label their political opposition as a physical threat or extremists or white supremacists or any other label that will simultaneously turn people against them while ignoring the argument of the opposition. We've seen a lot of leftist propaganda over the last several years. The sandman case, the Rittenhouse case, police shootings, riots that burn down cities attack police and occupy parts of cities.

All an attempt to destroy our legal system. We know what happened on January 6th and we know how the media and the left are portraying it. It is outrageous and sickening. It shows us the left, the media, and the feds were working together and against us. They have shown they do not wish to be one nation of one people anymore. They try to draw as much attention to the right, so no one sees what they have done. They'll focus on "right-wing extremists" and tell you what a threat they are. All the while leftwing extremists hold cities hostage, burn cities to the ground, terrorize people who stand up for what's right and disagree with them. If being an extremist means I oppose tyranny and love freedom, then I gladly accept the label. We are now a mob society in love with majority rule setting the stage for history to repeat itself. Like a bird with a broken wing, freedom cannot achieve what it is capable of if all standards are not met. We must ask ourselves, is this what self-rule looks like?

When two parties of people live together in a society, they both have their ideas on how things should be done and what should be done. Everyone wants things to go their way. There are three main ways a party can have things go their way, compromise, control, and separation. Compromise allows for a party to have things partially done their way and partially done their opponents way. When compromise is not an option there are two options that split off from compromise. One of the ways for a party to have it their way is by control. When a party no longer wants to compromise it may choose to go the villainous route and try and obtain power by controlling the other party. This is usually done by obtaining more power than the opposing party and then gradually taking away the people's freedoms. The second path split away from a lack of compromise in order to have things go your way is through separation. This is done either peacefully or violently. When things aren't going your way, and there is no hope for compromise, this option is the most logical and fair of the two options when done peacefully. When it is not done peacefully, it's usually due to the other party's oppression of the other and its refusal of the separation due to the fear of losing control over the separatist party. So, in this way separation and control forcibly split from one another as they are both void of compromise. In our society today, we are a party being controlled by the other as compromise is rarely seen. Leaving but one logical option for our future, separation.

Our nation and our freedoms are more fragile than anyone would like to believe. We like to believe we are stronger than we've ever been and virtually indestructible. The reality is that our nation and our freedoms are extremely fragile because we have the power and responsibility that comes with freedom and self-rule. If we continue to take the freedom without the responsibility of the power, then those far less responsible with power and far less caring of our freedom, will soon shatter the fragile foundational pillars of our nations values, fundamental principles of freedom, limited government and self-rule. One clumsy move in this glass fortress, and we lose it all. We are far too delicate to be playing reckless and deadly games by not taking action to prevent its demise.

"Freedom is never more than one generation away from extinction. We didn't pass it to our children in the bloodstream. It must be fought for, protected, and handed on for them to do the same, or one day we will spend our sunset years telling our children and our children's children what it was once like in the United States where men were free."

Ronald Reagan

Chapter 7
DIVISION

"Reason obeys itself; ignorance submits to whatever is dictated to it."

Thomas Paine

We are divided politically, culturally, religiously, and morally. We are also divided geographically, both nationally and urban vs rural, even more so as people attempt to escape oppressive states and cities. Our time period is also faced with a unique phenomenon. What's a no brainer to one group is absurd to the other. We can't even agree on the definition of words anymore. The differences of the human race are no longer language or nationality but those who can reason and think logically vs those who can't. We've always been divided by the decent vs the indecent, but that divide is taking a greater toll on society as the human race reaches its peak capability of organized civility. These two groups of the decent and logical vs the indecent and illogical are quickly becoming more and more alien to the other. Nations across the globe are also being agitated and torn apart by tyrannical leftist insanity. No matter your nation, don't let leftism destroy it. Be proud of who you are, your nation, and wave your nation's flag high and proud. If another world war is coming, it may not be fought between nations but within them.

Self-rule was a staple concept that led to the founding of this nation, but the greater the differences between us, the harder self-rule becomes, and survival becomes the name of the game. As Abraham Lincoln paraphrased from the Bible, "A house divided against itself cannot stand. Meant to inspire unity, it now inspires a different thought. If we can't unite, we must divide out of self-preservation.

<u>Financial Responsibility</u>

We want our tax dollars putting food on the table. We don't want taxes used for any of the absurd programs and policies that leftists want it going towards. Leftist politicians will give our tax dollars to other leftists through their programs and policies. Our military is now helping to pay for gender reassignment surgeries and hormone treatment. Which by the way is a double standard in multiple ways. No other members are allowed to be dependent on medications. No other members can choose which genders physical standards they want to meet, and no other members can have unnecessary surgeries paid for. Our military is becoming unrecognizable as the left strips the military of its focus on readiness and honor.

So, what else are they doing with your money? They give illegal immigrants special treatment over actual citizens and give them tens of millions of dollars in handouts in the form of prepaid credit cards. They allocated 4.1 billion dollars of your money to fund global safe spaces for transsexuals.

They give your money to Planned parenthood that is now handing out transition hormones to teens. They use your tax dollars in student loan forgiveness programs, making you pay for someone else's decisions. They are now paying for flights for illegal immigrants. They give your money to terrorists and our enemies in the form of humanitarian aid, all while knowing it will just end up being used to fuel the enemies' cause. But these aren't as ridiculous as all the leftist "research projects" that are also taxpayer funded and approved by congress. Most leftists don't even understand that government funded means taxpayer funded. Which is also why they struggle with concepts like inflation, and why a fat welfare system is bad for the economy, or why free health care and free education is illogical, or why socialism is ridiculous. They believe currency holds no real value and can be printed off indefinitely. When they destroy the economy, they lie to our faces telling us we are not financially suffering because of the economy, and the economy is doing great. They then blame their economic failures on "Shrink-flation," as in companies not lowering prices when production costs are said to go down. They're always blaming corporate greed for the economic troubles people are experiencing after they destroy the economy with their policies. Biden's term in office from 2020-2024 alone added more to our national debt than our nation's total costs of World War 2. This added to the trillions already added to our debt from Covid. Today our national debts interest payments alone are nearly equal to our nation's GDP, leading to an economic collapse.

<u>Reasoning</u>

"To argue with a person who has renounced the use of reason is like administering medicine to the dead."

Thomas Paine

What leftists see as a financial priority reveals to the rest of us their mental stability and ability to reason. But the madness doesn't end there. At the very least leftists are childish and crazy enough to go around vandalizing or stealing political yard signs they are offended by. They want trans men in women's sports, bathrooms, and Prisons. They have an irrational loyalty to the worst president in history who also has dementia and is an embarrassment to this country, all because they don't like Donald Trump for reasons they can't come up with. Their irrational loyalty goes further to support the scummiest, most corrupt and hypocritical politicians, simply because they like one stance the person has. They vote for more government, and then when more government does more damage, they vote for even more government to try to solve the problems that more government created in the first place. They try to fight poverty with high taxes. As in they raise taxes to provide government assistance for those in need which ends up taxing more people into poverty which creates more people needing government assistance which further raises taxes perpetuating the cycle. We have government and businesses helping to pay for abortions and transition surgeries. We have business discriminating against white employees and favoring minorities. You no longer must be qualified for the job position, you just need to not be straight, white, Christian, or a man. They will label others what they clearly are. You don't like me because I'm white? Now who's racist? You don't like me because I'm a man? Now who's sexist? You don't like me because I'm heterosexual? Look who's a heterophobe. You don't like me because I'm a conservative Christian? Now who's bigoted.

They are the most insane and hysterical among us. There's so much insanity occurring so fast it drowns out other insanity, that too few people are outraged by anything that they should be anymore. Leftists don't even present logical arguments if any at all. They think and debate subjectively instead of through a more rational objective thinking process. They think with their emotions and not their brains. They don't have rebuttals, they just know they feel how they feel and can't figure out why you don't see things their way so they just lash out like a child and start calling you names, and label you as a hateful person in order to avoid the argument and try to understand why you think the way you do. The worst part is they don't reflect on the fact they don't have an argument or wonder if they might be incorrect in their conclusions. They are the masters of circular reasoning on most issues, especially when it comes to their denial of reality such as the defining of genders. To top off the damage done, they look back on all they have done and honestly believe they are doing a great job.

How is it that we can observe the same thing and arrive at such vastly different conclusions? If you asked a conservative how they view the MAGA movement they might say it is steering America in a much-needed direction at a very critical time, and that it only makes sense to put America and Americans first. It is a common sense, grassroots movement. If you asked a leftist the same question they might say, it is a racist, hateful, white supremacist Nazi movement. So how is it that the left arrives at these extremely different conclusions? It's obvious in their response. It's an emotional response to something they are threatened by. They are no longer capable of forming a rational opinion. I would further argue that those who call themselves moderates but support the leftist madness movement by continuing to vote for democrats, are in fact just as extreme for doing so. The age of reason and understanding has passed after Democrats "drew first blood" by ignorantly labeling their opposition as racists, homophobes, bigots, etc. As well as ignoring the point of view of the opposing side, jumping to conclusions and not trying to understand why we believe what we believe. Democrats are the pawns of the leftist elites, helping to achieve their extremist agendas. If you're not part of the solution, you're part of the problem. One extreme sometimes requires another.

If we are expected to be a united people, I'd ask in what way are we now united? Can a union of marriage between two people succeed or even function if the two are from such vastly different worlds with nothing in common and every foundational belief opposite of each other? How is it even worth trying to make it work? Your efforts of unity are wasted and better put to use building a new life of your own, void of the opposition.

Debates between us and them are no longer debates, but arguments. Irrational arguments that go around in circles and yield no conclusion, progress, understanding, or compromise. They cannot be reasoned with. There are no compromises, only power struggles. Progress cannot be achieved under such circumstances, only regression and deterioration. The divide, like a crack in a damn only further widens until the damn breaks. How much is too much? We must separate before the damn breaks. If not for our prosperity, then for our preservation.

Foreign Affairs

The left's foreign policies have created many monsters that will soon grow too large for our nation and our allies to be able to handle. Such as future problems caused by illegal immigrants in general but also illegal immigrant sanctuary cities gaining more representatives and electoral votes due to their population increase. Leftists believe in securing other nations' borders before our own. They do not believe in a peace through strength strategy, they believe in peace through giving in to our enemies' demands. They are better to our enemies then our allies and better to our allies then the American people. They even have little if any respect for our veterans. They give up strategic positions, resources, technologies, and deals. We will never forget the debacle of the Afghanistan withdrawal. They create terrorist organizations such as Isis and Hezbollah. They fund and arm terrorists directly or indirectly. They fund and allow our enemies development of nuclear weapons. Their weak approach to our enemies emboldens them to take action, and attack and invade our allies and other nations. It almost seems like they are trying to reignite the cold war, start World War three, and accelerate the growth of terrorist groups.

The democratic party has become a threat to our national security. Through their rewriting of history, leftists have convinced themselves of falsehoods that take us further into their upside-down world as they become more and more sympathetic towards terrorists such as Hamas, in the Gaza/Israeli war. They blame Israel, our ally, after Israel is attacked, and they ignore the atrocities of Hamas. Siding with terrorists that brutally slaughter and torture children and babies, as well as siding against our ally is a position that should make leftists *the real enemy*.

Our nation is currently suffering from a severe identity crisis. It causes internal turmoil, our enemies to think we are a joke, and our allies find it difficult to trust us. What does it mean to be an American these days? Who are we? Can we even define ourselves anymore? If we can't answer these questions, we can't solve our problems and we can't build a future for our nation. When a division of any kind occurs, the victorious side will be the one preserving what little identity this nation has left. Preservation of our nation's flag, symbols and monuments is absolutely critical. The greatest weakness of the leftist minded is that they never have an identity, as they go in any direction the wind blows and are not anchored in any belief or principle culturally, socially, morally, or politically.

<u>False Hope</u>

Can't we all just get along? Let's just talk it out and hug it out. These feel good, seemingly hopeful suggestions of unity and compromise are just that. They make us feel good. They are the Anti doom and gloom wishful thinking that our emotions crave. But they are delusional, illogical and impractical. This concept of just putting aside our differences and talking things out in order to work together in perfect peace and harmony does work but only on an individual level and is only temporary. All human beings have the ability to connect with each other over what makes us human and what we have in common. But once the dazzle of small talk and feel-good talk wears off, and people are forced to live, work and survive amongst each other, reality sets in. Compromise is possible when two or more parties have few major differences and are not attempting to decide something major that dictates something for everyone. You can debate all day with someone and even win at every turn in a debate with them, but if you don't agree on basic fundamentals, you will not sway their opinion on a single matter of any significance.

The phrase "Reach across the aisle" is often used in political debates in elections to see how willing a candidate is to "work with" and compromise with the other side to achieve some form of progress. The lefts candidates refuse to compromise in the slightest on anything anymore. We have polarized to two complete opposite stances on everything that most compromises are not even remotely possible. Such as yes or no decisions in government. So what do we have to reach across the aisle to? Open borders? Betrayal of our allies? Taking away our gun rights? Tyrannical government? Inability to protect our families and property? The murder of the unborn innocent? Purely insane proposals, policy's, expenses, laws, action and inaction?

They have made one thing very clear; we are their enemy. No compromise, just attack after attack keeping us on defense while they gain ground. If we are to be their enemy, we must start acting like it if we want to win anything. We need to be on offense taking the fight to them. We need to propose the extreme and let them try to talk us down to a compromise if they can. A "National Divorce" may be our only solution and our only hope. At this point our differences have created too large of a division between us to fill, and the gap only grows wider with time. We have created far too many issues for ourselves as the first world problems of a whiny and spoiled society are never ending. Like bickering children, too many look to the government to be our parent to settle the matter for us.

Some ask, "But what of all the hope we see in those on the left siding with the right on the big issues? Isn't there hope for converting leftists?" Any idiot can see fire as a bad thing and want to stop it, but the problem isn't the fire, the problem is the idiot. The idiot might try to put out the fire with more fuel. The idiot will never wonder how the fire started in the first place or how to avoid it from happening again. The idiot may learn to put out the fire, but only to start a new one later. When democrats come over to the republican party, they aren't undergoing a magical transition to believe what we believe with complete understanding. They have simply decided they no longer wish to be associated with the leftist extremists running this country due to their stance on at least one issue. By doing so they have only created an illusion of party numbers in government. This diluting of our party has been going on for some time now and they are known as RINOs or Republicans in name only. This is what is weighing down our parties' accomplishments and potential. Without our foundational beliefs and the ability and willingness to reason, there is no hope. This is not defeatism; this is the opposite. The acceptance of our reality is what gives us hope. By cutting loose the ball and chain that hold us back, we can finally be free to truly prosper.

Some among us have held on to the idea that a nation requires two opposites to balance each other out, relating it to a bird with two wings, a left wing and right wing. On the surface this may sound profound, but a little further thought exposed how idiotic this thought really is. Just like with a bird's wings, each must flap and turn in coordination with each other in order to make the bird fly, and in an agreed upon direction and speed. We may have had this at one point in time, but now we are more like a bird with two heads that flaps erratically, cannot stay a flight, and will only succeed at tearing itself apart in its efforts to fly in opposite directions.

Today we are arguably as divided as Israelis and Palestinians, seemingly literally as the war divides at home. If you feel like every policy the democratic party tries to advance is nearly an act of war, you're not alone. The left grows more and more radical and is only building momentum. Do not think for a second they will be stopped by a great victory in an election. Wins in elections only buy us a little more time. We can barely hold them off with our slim majorities, if we can even maintain one. No matter the victories, no matter the 2024 election outcome, **this will not stop.**

There is a time for a culture to adapt and evolve, and there is a time for a culture to survive. Should we not draw a line for any political beliefs or agendas? Especially for those holding public office? We should obviously be open to all ideas and views, but what if those people and their views show a complete lack of understanding of what makes this nation functional and thriving? What if they don't understand our nation's founding principles that make America what it is? What if their intent is to harm our country? Do we make no attempt to preserve ourselves as all other nations do? After the Revolutionary war, many of the loyalists stayed and prospered from what they fought against, as well as the racist democratic party after the civil war being allowed to continue and cause chaos and division. They raised their children to think the same way as them, and after decades of this, and illegal immigrants not assimilating, and allowing our children to be indoctrinated by European socialist and Marxist failed ideas and principles, here we are today, ready for yet another civil war as the left continue to rebel against the United States. A former enemy allowed to reside within a nation, is a festering open wound. We can continue to boil ourselves in hate, anger, frustration and dark thoughts, or we can free each other from each other's burden. It's becoming difficult to tell the difference between the left and our enemies overseas. We seem to have more in common with like-minded people from other nations than our own fellow citizens. Perhaps the new age of human civilization will yield a dual polarity of human society, splitting the world in two as we can see the possibility of a global civil war on the horizon. We have reached our peak and now our nation is in decline. The time to split is now. If weak men create bad times and strong men create good times, then let weak men have their own nation to destroy and let strong men have their own nation to prosper. We call ourselves the United States, but what are we actually united in as a people if not even the prosperity of the nation?

<u>Politics and Political Bias</u>

Leftists will continue to agitate by ignoring their opposition and falsely labeling their opponents. They make average right leaning citizens out to be crazy racist old white men. Or are we actual citizens with actual concerns we are trying to voice while not being allowed to.

There used to be a sense of pride and dignity in the Whitehouse and in the federal government, but any resemblance of such is long gone. The democratic party has been responsible for scandal after sex scandal in DC for several decades now. Recently: drugs found in the Whitehouse, Tik Tok tours by transsexual and drag queens, and now sex tapes being made by congressional staffers in the Senate office building. Even something as embarrassing as a Representative pulling a fire alarm like a child to avert a government shutdown and then lying about it. Even our state governments are being disgraced, to say the least. A satanic alter was set up in the state capital of Idaho, and it was shown to have been done "legally." At the same time the Ten commandments had to be removed from many state capital buildings. Even small disrespectful moves are being done to our capital buildings, such as in the state of Wisconsin, the governor decided it was a good idea to put up a "science tree" instead of a Christmas tree in an effort to disrespect and antagonize Christians. Democrats have been and continue to be a disgrace and embarrassment to our nation for the whole world to see. Yet they still make a big deal about Nixon when he at least had the decency to resign. We have seen the damage a fool of a leftist president can do to our country, just imagine what can and will happen when a more serious, cognitively functional person with a more aggressive leftist agenda would do.

The election integrity of the democratic party is almost nonexistent with gerrymandering, ballot fraud, not requiring IDs, and attempting to control elections by either stopping opponents from being able to run or keeping the opposition off the ballot. A cold civil war in this country has already begun as we can even see political discrimination in the workplace and in our education system. The democratic party winning elections used to just disappoint us, but today it scares the hell out of us. With zero compromise from democrats, we are sure to see an increase in the number of government shutdowns that delay any political progress. This has led to the states attempting to take matters into their own hands as the leftist majority in the federal government refuse to act on federal issues such as the border crisis. The federal government's power trip with the state of Texas attempting to secure its border has led to the inevitable division and resistance of "Red" states standing up to the oppressive and incompetent federal government. The leftists started the "Not my President" movement with Trump, perhaps it's time we adopt a similar attitude. How long will it be until right wing and left-wing governors and mayors stop listening to the other side's authority and start listening to their own side's authority? Will states begin to form defense pacts with each other in the future? Could this be the way we end up splitting up the country? Is this how we would really want it to happen?

We have been witnessing the political weaponization of the FBI through our new double standard justice system targeting the left's political opponents. Attacking candidates and party members alike. In the heavily dramatized Jan 6th protest, or so called "insurrection" or "end of democracy" or "attack on the capital" agents seeded themselves in our protests as they no doubt often do. They try to rile up the crowd in hopes their friends in the media will be given a propaganda jackpot. The leftist long dreamed of American Police State is well underway.

A pattern of the effects of those in power has emerged with an idiotic interpretation from leftists. When the left is in power the economy goes to hell, so they blame the Republicans that were previously in power. When Republicans take power the economy rebounds, so the previous leftists that were in power take credit, claiming their policies had a "delayed reaction."

The covid19 pandemic has created another form of division, but not a natural one, an engineered one. Mandates in government, Airports and Healthcare facilities have filtered out those who love freedom and left behind the ignorant, complacent, leftist cult followers. This is setting the stage for a great conflict if such an event were to occur again.

The left is becoming ever more aggressive in their fight to reconstruct America in their image. They have been fiercely attacking the electoral college for decades. In their quest for a majority rule direct democracy, they have been forming what is known as the NPVIC or National Popular Vote Interstate Compact. It is essentially an election political defense pact between leftist controlled states vowing to cast all their electoral votes for the winner of the majority vote in an effort to circumvent the electoral college, provided enough electoral votes are promised to be able to win. This is an aggressive attack on our nation's founding and an aggressive takeover of our nation's presidential elections which will result in an armed conflict. The electoral college is the primary mechanism for ensuring all our states in our union are equally represented in presidential elections. The left wishes to do away with this which will destroy our union and give the leftist run major cities complete power over the rest of us in every future presidential election. Of all the grave leftist threats to our nation's future, NPVIC is one I find especially and uniquely frightening.

(During the publication of this book, an assassination attempt on our former president and presidential candidates life was made. Whether or not the shooter acted alone or was put up to the task, one thing is clear; this is a symptom of a greater disease, the tip of the iceberg. The left has been manufacturing dangerous, emotionally unstable extremists through media indoctrination, fear mongering, filtering information, and spreading false stories and accusations. All to create as negative of a perspective of Trump as possible, to stealthily insight violence by enraging their viewers to the point of taking drastic measures. The media and the elitists pulling the strings have intentionally done this and tortured this man since the day he started running for political office. Through spreading lies, they have made him run a gauntlet of attacks and mastered legal defamation of their political opponent. From painting him as a racist to calling him a Hitler equivalent to the Russia collusion hoax to two impeachment attempts to multiple political prosecution to removing him from the ballot to trying to jail him and now he has been shot and nearly killed. And yet, I believe they will never stop forcing us to listen to their ludicrous rant of how they believe January 6th was the worst thing to happen to this country thanks to the terrible Republicans. Or maybe they will use this tragedy to try and paint themselves as the peaceful heroes that all of a sudden want nothing more than unity in this country, while they quietly stab us in the back every chance they have. That is until things cool down again and then they will be right back at it again, calling us a threat to democracy, and domestic terrorists.)

An armed conflict this nation is quickly and inevitably heading toward must be avoided as much as reasonably possible. But we are running out of time to take peaceful steps to avoid such a conflict. The left has positioned themselves to have encircled us with their fingers on multiple triggers that at any moment could become the igniting catalyst in an unstoppable chain reaction of violent events. From tensions at the border, to problems caused by illegal immigrants, to a violation of the 2nd Amendment, to a result of the national debt, to another destructive infuriating foreign policy disaster, to the democratic party's election NPVIC National Popular Vote Interstate Compact.

The pro Hamas campus protests as of late have only proved many of my previously mentioned predictions true. Primarily, that things will not get better but only worse. As well as leftists' inability to reason and think for themselves. And of course you get to pay for their students' loan debt forgiveness. Instead of "defund the police," perhaps we should de-fund our universities. Take any of the latest political news and ask yourself, would this sort of thing happen in a nation void of leftism? Ask yourself; is this what self-rule looks like? This political tug of war we are in isn't a tug of war to see who will win, it's a tug of war to find out when the rope will snap. They don't present an argument or have a stance that isn't a purely emotional ultimatum. Their ultimatum:

no debate, no compromise, no peace, do what we want or else!

Perhaps it's time for our ultimatum; *Division!* One way or another.

<u>The Fracture</u>

A major natural division among people has been the differences in the urban and rural way of life. Not only do certain types of people choose to live in one or the other, but the urban and rural life creates certain types of people. A rural/small town life can lead to a greater understanding of the value of private property, dependence on yourself for safety, housing, property maintenance, and transportation. Because of this independent mindset, rural/small town people believe in the defense of private property, love guns, and hate taxes. While an urban/big city life can lead to less of an understanding of the value of private property, a dependence on *government* for safety, housing, property maintenance, and transportation. Because of this dependent mindset, urban/big city people tend to not see defense of private property as that important, hate guns, and think taxes are a good thing. This may contribute heavily to why urban areas lean left, and rural areas lean right. Urban areas also see crime very differently than rural people as crime is part of everyday life in major cities. People who move from a city to the country may be in pursuit of lower taxes, fewer permits, and be willing to trade a life of amenities, comfort, and safety for a life of significantly more freedom. As differences between urban and rural areas become more obvious, people relocate or become indoctrinated by their surrounding culture. This allows big cities to become a petri dish for leftist ideas and agendas. Globalism, Big government, Socialism, Fascism, Communism, wokeism, extreme environmentalism, etc.

There are obviously two forms of division, the preferable one peaceful and the other a last resort of violence. The people of eastern Oregon have started an attempt at a peaceful division. Attempting to simply redraw state lines as has been done in this country many times before, though they have found themselves a bureaucratic nightmare to work through. The people of eastern Oregon are attempting to secede from western Oregon and join their neighboring state of Idaho in what is known as the Greater Idaho movement. Counties of northeastern California are attempting to join them as well. If it works others are sure to follow suit as they should. "Red" counties in Nevada could also join Idaho. Otherwise if there was to be a Greater Utah movement, Nevada counties could join it as an alternative. Red counties from Arizona, Colorado and New Mexico could also join. A Greater Iowa movement would allow red counties from Minnesota, Wisconsin and Illinois to join. Alabama or Florida could free red counties from Georgia. "Red" counties in Michigan could either join the Greater Iowa movement or a Greater Ohio movement. A Greater Ohio movement could also take in "red" counties from Pennsylvania. A Greater West Virginia movement could also take in "red" counties from Pennsylvania as well as Virginia and Maryland. If Pennsylvania joins a movement the adjacent northeastern states "red" counties could also join. Once a states "red" counties join an adjacent "red" state it would be easier for them to then separate to form new states so to not lose seats in the US senate.

If such an undertaking doesn't work, a great internal migration will surely happen in due time. This would create a state vs state aggressive national political divide not seen since the Civil War. It seems somewhat simple to just pack up and move if life is really that bad in your state, but this is illogical as the geographical political division in most states is an urban/rural split not a state vs state split. Many states see one or two major cities carry the entire state in every election, leading to frustration from the desperation of those with rural political alignment. Any political map of the last decade will show urban areas leaning left and everywhere else leaning right. Along with taking elections, and breeding crime, big cities also dictate law and policy to the rest of the state. Oppressing those on the right to desperation. Desperation is the catalyst of war. Why should an archipelago of blue rule over a red continent? Swing states or "battle ground states" especially would be very wise to allow their cities or their rural counties to secede in order to benefit both sides, ease tensions and avoid a civil war.

Example 1

War or peaceful secession most likely will not create a state vs. state scenario as seen during the Civil War as there are actually no truly "blue" or "red" states. As previously mentioned, highly populated major cities carry the entire state in every presidential election, as all electoral votes of a state go to the candidate with the majority of electoral votes. I'm not in any way suggesting we scrap the electoral college as it is **essential to our republic**, but rather I'm suggesting we upgrade or adapt it to our nation's current political demographics with our modern extreme polarity in mind.

But what if each region of a state had their fair say in every presidential election? Just as congressional delegation is split through districts, the District Method allows a state's electoral votes to be divided among the presidential candidates, giving the candidates the number they actually won. The Congressional District Method uses the same one electoral vote per district as the standard winner takes all electoral college, and the winner of the state-wide vote receives the state's remaining two electoral votes from having two senators. Maine and Nebraska already use this method. But this isn't a cure-all as many major frustrations would remain, such as senatorial and gubernatorial elections as well as accurate representation and the problem of gerrymandering.

Example 2

Perhaps a new form of the district method could be created to use the same benefits of the district method while fixing at least the accurate representation and gerrymandering problems. District creation could be created prioritizing political representation alongside equal population representation. New district lines would be drawn through existing districts to separate "red" from "blue" as accurately as possible. These new districts would encompass a region's already existing political super majority and reduce minority numbers in each district that they would never be able to win in anyway. The minority would be regrouped into adjacent existing districts with people that share the same political affiliation. In other words, a 49% minority would shift to percentages of less than 20% as well as increasing majorities from 51% to 80% and greater. Unlike the Congressional District Method, the two remaining electoral votes from the states senators wouldn't be given to the majority, but rather one given to the party whose physical portion size of the state is greater, and one to the party of the current governor. This is to properly represent the state in the Union as senators are intended for.

This results firstly, in greater political autonomy for all people.

Secondly, fewer people belonging to the political minority would be misrepresented by their political opposition.

Thirdly, if electoral votes were divided between candidates, each new Congressional district would be able to give their own electoral vote to their presidential candidate in the most undeniably accurate fair representative way.

Fourthly, State representative district lines would be drawn to fit perfectly within Congressional districts, and a state or federal law would be passed to make the redrawing of red/blue adjacent district lines illegal. This the new law plus the fact that no manipulative political advantage would result from redrawing adjacent district lines of the same political affiliation, would result in the complete disabling of any gerrymandering ability or incentive from those in state power.

Fifthly, this new system would greatly ease political tensions.

Sixthly, ballot fraud would make almost no difference as the political majority in each district would be much greater and harder to overtake fraudulently.

Seventhly, in this new system third parties would finally have a real chance of electing a Congressional representative, as the local parties would no longer be extremely divided by left and right, but rather by minor disagreements of what priorities should be. Once a separation of any form occurs within this country, opportunities for third parties will finally open up.

Example 3

Option 1- A redrawing of state lines as with the greater Idaho movement, would buy us more time by solving most current issues. It could be done just like the greater Idaho movement where counties unite and break away from blue counties to join the nearest adjacent red state. But this should happen simultaneously or rapidly across the nation and not slowly state by state. Just as with the events leading up to the civil war, with the creation of new states, becoming pro-slavery or anti-slavery, having federal supervision. Although as history has shown us, the federal government at the time was unable to get out in front of the coming events leading to bleeding

Kansas. Let history be our guide so we do not repeat it. We would be creating new states and must ensure an even political division so not to give either party the upper hand in the federal government that they don't already have. Additionally, some "red" states and their "red" counties don't have an adjacent "red" state or "red" states county to be able to join. Alaska and Hawaii don't have any adjacent states. These factors mean the state may need to split into two or more states which would result in the creation of additional senators. Which again means this process must be carefully federally "supervised" to achieve fairness.

Option 2-Version A.- Another way of redrawing state lines would be to do it as accurately as possible. The redrawing of state lines should be drawn while focusing on red/blue areas within a county instead of by county lines as with the greater Idaho movement. Only minor changes to congressional district lines may be needed. What we have is an archipelago of blue in a sea of red. So, what we would end up with would be large, low population density red states and small high population density blue states. This formation of blue states that are cities would resemble the ancient Greek city states. The number of red states formed would be based on the number of blue states formed as they must be equal during this national transition in order to be equally represented in the union in the form of the senate. Red states could either keep the current general boundary lines or if they must divide, they could allow each other to have an equal number of congressional districts to be fair to one another with regional electoral representation in elections.

Option 2-Version B.- One possible way to accomplish this same concept of separation into the formation of city-state like governance is to go about it from a county level. In other words a county could split into two, one urban one rural. This would be less effective but may solve some big problems in your county and help to ease local tensions. Due to greater population in cities than the rest of the county the city would have to initiate this or the county would only be able to kick out smaller cities. This isn't ideal but may be much easier to accomplish in certain circumstances. The general idea is if it can't be done on one level of government, perhaps it could be done on another level.

Example 4

A complete separation into two different nations would be another possible theoretical solution. This solution would have two theoretical options. Two nations completely separate, or two nations conjoined in some form. Option A- As these new nations would be marbled together, a complete separation of the two nations in my opinion would not be physically possible or legislatively, economically, or militarily practical.

Option B- Our second option being two nations conjoined in some form, would have two different scenarios itself. Option B- Scenario A- The first is less preferable as it is more difficult and complex creating a significant potential for much to go wrong.

It would have a sort of Athens/Sparta relationship feel to it or a "sui generis" unique political relationship. Two independent nations, each with their own federal government. Separate by law and legislation. United in the partnership of sustaining a military and having a single currency. United only by the bare minimum standards for a functioning global region. But this scenario would share many of the same problems as option A of two completely separate nations although being far less complex and therefore much more feasible.

Option B- Scenario B- The second scenario of this second option of two nations conjoined in some form, is my personal favorite having few problems, simplicity and which fundamentals have already been proven. Much like something resembling Native American reservations or even more so a Commonwealth, such as Puerto Rico and the Northern Mariana Islands. Democrat super majority run major cities could become nations of city states within a nation. These ancient Greek style city states would function as their own independent nations but would be required to pay tribute to the United States for military protection. They would obviously use the same currency but as their own nation, they are not influenced by the federal laws of the United States just as the United States are not influenced by their laws. This option of course would require leftist cities to secede from the union, which can be done peacefully or by force, whichever choice the future may make for us. I would imagine as much as they seem to loathe everything about America, they would find it all too easy to willfully and peacefully exit if given the opportunity. As much as we are disgusted by them, they are also disgusted by us. They are disgusted with our sense of morality, our sense of reality, our compassion for the innocent, love for our children, love for our country, love of freedom, our self-reliant mindset, our work ethic, our economic common sense, and our inability to be compliant. So let us free them from our sanity, stability, and our contributions to society, and leave them to their rot and decay they lust after so fiercely.

From separating on an economic level, to separating within a state, to areas of a state separating, to our nation separating either by state, region or urban and rural; there are many ways to separate at many different levels for many different severity situations. We as a people must start the planning, preparations, and directional momentum in order to prevent civil war and to preserve what we can of the Union, ourselves, our culture, history, ideas, freedoms, and founding principles, before it's too late and time decides for us.

These ideas are meant to be suggestions or the beginning of an answer and not to be taken as the complete and final answer to any severity of any situation. Ideas are just drops in a bucket for whoever will collect them and make the best use of them. Some of these scenarios and options may just have their place and moment in time for at least some consideration. If some, even still, are too drastic for your liking, the future may just have you return to them for a more serious reconsideration.

Our founders knew that in order for the freedoms self-rule provides us with to survive, our strategies to self-rule would need to adapt and evolve to our ever-changing circumstances. America is not a nation or even a people, it is a concept. A concept with the ability to survive. If we have the courage to let it survive. As we stand on the shoulders of giants, we see how far our founders have taken us and we hope their wisdom can take us just a little bit further to assist us in laying the final bricks of our great nation.

A World Without Them

Our founding fathers gave us a nation that allows us to make necessary changes in order to better ourselves and better rule ourselves. We don't have to live in a chaotic, stressed and divided situation like this. Imagine a version of this country in which the left had no influence or impact on us, on our livelihood, on our young children, on our economy, on our laws and legislation, on our constitution, on our government, our military, our morality and culture, on our foreign affairs, on our nation's security, on our education system and science, on our history and founding principles, on our justice, on our freedom. A nation in which we are properly represented and capable of self-rule as our founding fathers intended. Compare the many great reasons to separate with the lesser few reasons to stay connected to our parasite, and the contrast makes the latter argument hardly worth our time and breath to discuss it. Democrats almost seem to be using a playbook on how to destroy America with every goal of theirs being the complete opposite of how to make a nation flourish. Democrats aren't playing by the rules of how our government was meant to function. Instead, they lie, cheat, steal, and most of all wage cultural warfare against us to try and circumvent the proper channels of political change.

Great change does not happen overnight, but rather slowly over time. In this way they trend farther left and the push off the cliff remains undetectable and unassuming. However, a close examination of its pattern can reveal what its future will look like. The future of leftism is void of freedom and reason. Separation is imminent. Our fellow countrymen could become our enemy if we do not take immediate action to separate ourselves from provoking oppression.

Are you frightened by the idea of a political restructuring of our nation? I'm frightened of a future where the people did nothing to stop tyranny from consuming freedom and American principles. A future where our nation is unrecognizable from its founding. A nation that has completely rewritten history and turned our schools into re-education camps. A nation that abandons its allies and makes itself vulnerable to its enemies. A nation with backwards justice. A nation whose laws have turned against its own citizens.

I'm frightened by the inevitability that if we do nothing, there won't be much of an America left to save. I'm afraid of the America our children will grow up in and inherit. I'm afraid a future of inaction will trade a future of maximum potential and prosperity, for a future of desperation and struggle.

Our nation is in a very terrifying position right now. Things will not get better, only worse. Our divide will only further widen. America will inevitably divide. But will it divide orderly or chaotically? Will it divide through peace or war? Let us separate peacefully, before the inevitable bad times up ahead require the lives of good men to get us out of them. The term division or secession when heard by anyone would and should create a sense of fear and for good reason. The last time such words were uttered, events unraveled very tragically for our nation and its people. At the time of the Civil War the truth was that our nation needed to stay unified in order to survive. Today, we must divide to survive. Things are different now; our nation's threats have taken on a different form and use different tactics. We are under attack on all fronts from a parasite within. It's time to salvage what we can and cut our losses.

We love this country, and we want what's best for it. We are not about kicking people out of our country for being different then us or different then the majority, but it is our duty to rid ourselves of those who are so lacking in understanding of the concepts, of self-rule, freedom, and our founding principles, that they attack such concepts without hesitation. If America falls, our world allies fall. And any idea the world ever had of freedom dies and is lost forever. We must divide to survive.

Chapter 8
LIBERTY OR DEATH

"Give me liberty or give me death!"

Patrick Henry

"The God who gave us life, gave us liberty at the same time; the hand of force may destroy, but cannot disjoin them."

Thomas Jefferson

When there is nothing we can do through peaceful means to save our country, our rights, our way of life, what is the alternative? What are we to do?

War; the final option for division. If we choose what we know, and do nothing to stop the inevitable, war will come, and we may not have time to control the manner in which it arrives.

A life without freedom is not a life worth living. But a life with freedom is a life worth dying for. Standing up to bullies and tyrants isn't just an American thing it is a human characteristic. People have always fought against oppressors since the beginning. The oppression of an invading army has always been worth fighting against. The oppression of your own government, even more so.

External or internal oppressors both have one main thing in common. They both become unwelcome occupiers. Freedom fighters have always worked together with those from other nations, cultures, languages, and religious beliefs to take down their common enemy. Whether it's a Pharaoh, a Caesar, a King, a Dictator, or a Mob, good men must stand together to fight all the wrong and unjust in this world.

"The duty of a true Patriot is to protect his country from its government."

Thomas Paine

"War is when the government tells you who the bad guy is. Revolution is when you decide that for yourself."

Benjamin Franklin

"What country can preserve its liberties if its rulers are not warned from time to time that their people preserve the spirit of resistance? Let them take arms."

Thomas Jefferson

<u>April Morning</u>

April 19, 1775, 5 o'clock in the morning, 77 men stood against 400 in defiance of tyranny. Men of different ethnicity, race, class, religion and age, stood shoulder to shoulder prepared to sacrifice all they hold dear, without any concern of the end result. The use of their own blood and lives to be used as protest against tyranny, in hopes it would echo throughout all of time. The shot heard round the world.

These men weren't expecting much if anything for reinforcements, but after hearing what had happened, their fellow patriot countrymen started pouring in over the hills to rain down on the British troops. From 77 men at the first shot, to nearly 500 to chase the British back to Boston. By the time the British retreat had reached Boston, Patriot numbers had swollen to nearly 4000 strong.

Who among us today I wonder, will be the next 77 when needed?

As for those who remain content and undisturbed with the winds of change. You are content with your chains. Content with being slaves. Content with your true potential and prosperity being taken from you. Content with your best life becoming the, "what could have been" life. You believe you should be ruled, instead of ruling yourselves. To you your chains equal peace, and peace you will have; a peaceful ignorance, a peaceful slavery. "I prefer dangerous freedom over peaceful slavery" Thomas Jefferson

<u>Guns</u>

"Oppressors can tyrannize only when they achieve a standing army, an enslaved press, and a disarmed populace."

James Madison

"Political power grows out of the barrel of a gun."

Mao Zedong.

"The most foolish mistake we could possibly make would be to allow the subjugated races to possess arms."

Adolf Hitler.

What power does the common man possess other than the rifle in his hands? History has shown us that in the events leading up to a tyrannical takeover, civilian owned firearms have always been first in the sights of the majority and last before the takeover to be outlawed and confiscated.

The American Revolution started during large firearm confiscation raids leading up to 1775. Other examples include: Ottoman Empire 1911, Soviet Union 1929, Nazi Germany 1938, Communist China 1935, Cambodia 1956. The United States has been slowly tightening its grip on guns through legislation over the years. Hundreds of millions of innocent people have died by the hands of their own government as a result of gun confiscation.

Yet people remain ignorant and trusting of their governments no matter the situation. Most people always choose immediate satisfaction over long-term satisfaction. This always has catastrophic consequences.

The importance of firearms was stressed by George Washington on multiple occasions when he stated, "Fire arms stand next in importance to the constitution itself." and "A free, people ought not only be armed and disciplined, but they should have sufficient arms and ammunition to maintain a status of independence from any who might attempt to abuse them, which would include their own government." As well as "When government takes away citizens right to bear arms it becomes citizens' duty to take away governments' right to govern."

Americans, in general, seem to have passed down through generations the importance of firearms. Today, it is estimated that there are well over 450 million civilian owned firearms in the United States with 332 million citizens. In WW2, Japanese Admiral Isoroku Yamamoto was quoted saying, "You cannot invade the mainland United States. There would be a rifle behind every blade of grass."

With a gun, an individual possess power over their own physical life, the power to preserve freedom from tyranny, the freedom and power to protect yourself and your family from any threat, and the freedom and power in whatever life scenario to choose your own ending. As long as I still have breath in my lungs and a gun in my hand, I am free.

"Abraham Lincoln may have freed all Americans, but Samuel Colt made them all equal."

Anonymous

"When any nation mistrusts its citizens with guns, it is sending a clear message. It no longer trusts its citizens because such a government has evil plans."

George Washington

Amendment II- A well-regulated **militia**, being **necessary** to the security of a free state, the right of the people to **keep and bear arms**, <u>**shall not be infringed.**</u>

"When the people fear their government, there is tyranny; When the government fears the people, there is liberty."

Thomas Jefferson

US citizens do not possess a "well-regulated militia" as we should, that is so necessary to the security of a free state. We need local militias in every town and county. Militias need arsenals to include military vehicles, armored troop transports, and yes, even weapons on par with current military standards that are not accessible to the individual, but the militia as a whole. We have once again been asking ourselves the wrong question. Instead of asking ourselves how do we limit our citizens' military capability? We should be asking ourselves; how do we safely and securely arm our citizens to the maximum capability to do as the second amendment and our founders intended?

Our right to keep and bear arms has been consistently infringed on over the last one hundred years and continues to be more severely infringed upon every year. You can't have this you can't have that; you can't do that you can't do this; you can't take it here you can't take it there; you must have this; you must have that. That looks scary, you shouldn't have that. That sounds scary, you shouldn't have that. The gun committed the crime, the law-abiding citizen is the problem and the threat, laws stop crime because criminals will follow our laws. It's better this way, it's for our safety, it's for the children. Other countries don't have guns. No other country is as gun crazed as we are. That's not needed for hunting. That's not needed for self-defense. Your crazy for thinking the governments a threat. Why do you need this? Why do you need that? Why so many guns? Why so much ammo? *Explain to <u>me</u>*, why you should have those guns?

The second amendment is essentially a breath saver. In other words, the second amendment exists so that we don't have to explain to anyone why it and our other rights and freedoms should exist. They are God given inalienable rights.

Our local rural law enforcement has been tested time and time again to see if they will enforce tyrannical law. Most have passed and chose to defend the constitution. But how long I wonder can they hold out? If you oppose the constitution, you oppose America and its people. Making you an enemy of the United States. We must be far less tolerant and forgiving with enemies on our own turf.

An attempt to take away our firearms will without a doubt trigger a revolt, just as it did in 1775. Will we be ready?

<u>Inevitability</u>

What is a Patriot to do when half his country sees the Constitution as something up for debate, to interpret loosely or to dismiss entirely? The administrative State, infinitely funded by the Federal Reserve, the unelected writing legislation circumventing congress makes this nation unrecognizable from its founding. Now's the time to act as generations able to see the contrast between the America with freedom and the America that lost freedom. The next generations will become content with their familiarity with the prison of a nation they are in. Aggression can be a good thing. Lack of aggression leads to complacency. Our society has been conditioning us to be less aggressive and more complacent. Like a dog that has had the wolf bred out of him over time, we are now loyal, obedient pups, too timid to bite back and rip our abusers to shreds.

Despite our most desperate attempts to avoid war, I fear it will find us sooner rather than later during our clumsy attempts to maintain unity in a nation that is already divided. Do we have less in common with each other than Israelis and Palestinians? Or any other two groups that have gone to war with each other? When it comes to our most passionate fundamentals, opposites *do not* attract. Our equally passionate polarity is like two magnets with the same powerful polarities facing one another. The harder some try to force us together, the more aggressively we fight to repel each other. How unwise it is to marry gunpowder and flame. If we do not peacefully separate, an explosive situation surely awaits us.

None the less to many will cling to the sinking ship of unity, in hopes their feel-good positivity will dismiss the reality of taking on water and propel us safely through the dark centuries to follow.

Preparations

"By failing to prepare, you are preparing to fail."
Benjamin Franklin

What's our time frame to expect war to break out? That's the scary thing it could be 15 years from now or it could be tomorrow. One law passed, one Supreme Court decision, or one more lockdown could easily trigger a violent reaction. From anyone. Even from yourself. We all must prepare for any and all scenarios to occur at any given time. Preparations including planning, stockpiling or securing resources, preparing for unavailability of vital resources including currency, coordinate efforts to convene and organize, prepare and plan for your immediate actions as well as your midterm and long-term actions. Keep communication lines short and simple, and circles of trust small. Prepare for the most likely scenario first. Then prepare for the worst-case scenario. Be ready to defend your freedoms, in any form that is required.

What They Did

Our nation's founding fathers laid out the perfect blueprint in attempts to prevent a war. Including boycotts, protests, petitioning oppression, forming an independent congress, pleading with the king to allow for a peaceful separation, and created a declaration of independence. The formed First Continental Congress was responsible for encouraging noncompliance with the Coercive Acts and declaring them to be unconstitutional. They organized boycotts of British goods. They prepared and encouraged local militias for the possibility of an armed conflict. They voted in favor of independence to move things forward. They influenced local courts to hear laws and cases independent from royal authority. They voted to encourage colonies to replace their royal governments with their own. Finally, they approved the Declaration of Independence.

<u>What They Went Through</u>

"These are the times that try men's souls. The summer soldier and the sunshine patriot will, in this crisis, shrink from the service of their country; but he that stands by it Now, deserves the love and thanks of man and woman. Tyranny, like hell, is not easily conquered; yet we have this consolation with us, that the harder the conflict, the more glorious the triumph."

Thomas Paine

The mindset of our Patriot ancestors deserves recognition and our attention. There have been few events in history where a people as debilitated as them chose to stand up to an opponent so mighty. An unformed, non-unified, region of ordinary people from all different backgrounds, chose to stand up to the mightiest empire in the world. Farmers, Saddlers, Brickman, lumberjacks, shoemakers, brewers, lawyers, tavern keepers, printers, barbers, teachers, merchants, carpenters, fishermen, blacksmiths, veterans. All concluded their options were liberty or death. They concluded, a life without freedom is not a life worth living.

From the beginning, outnumbered, out gunned, out trained, out maneuvered, out supplied, and out financed. At Breeds hill and New York, they faced impossible odds and an overly determined adversary. At Valley forge with inadequate apparel, they endured freezing temperatures that would cause severe frostbite and take the lives of many men. They faced starvation, disease, infection, and a long hopeless fight ahead. Men stepped up when and where needed. Especially during the creation of the Continental Navy and Marines. What guts it must have taken to be one of the first Continental ships to confront the most powerful Navy on earth. With a little creativity, strategy, and good Intel, they were able to turn the tide of battle at Fort Ticonderoga, Trenton, Princeton, Saratoga, Cowspen, and York Town.

"All men are afraid in battle. The coward is the one who lets his fear overcome his sense of duty."

General George S. Patton

Despite the odds, they understood that real soldiers are free men who fight for freedom. If you don't fight for freedom, you are not a soldier, but a slave. If the voices of our fallen and those who served freedom could still be heard today, no doubt they would tell us to earn and preserve what they sacrificed everything for. The free world they have passed down to us. To many have fought and died for us to just give it all up without a fight.

"It is foolish and wrong to mourn the men who died. Rather we should thank God such men lived."

General George S. Patton

Mindset

Our Patriot ancestors had the mindset necessary to fight and win a war. They understood what going to war meant. They considered and understood the horrors of war. They were prepared to sacrifice their lives. They were prepared to sacrifice everything. In this life, war is a part of human nature. War does not ever end; it just takes on a different form. Peace is just a war in slow motion. It moves so slow that it doesn't catch the eye's attention. We can't avoid war in this life, but we can choose the side we are on, we can choose what we will fight and die for. If you don't have anything worth dying for, then you don't have anything worth living for.

"There are but two parties now: traitors and patriots."
General Ulysses S. Grant

We must also have the proper mindset to treat a cultural cold war as seriously as a real war. Where is the outrage in this country from the right? Some have lit themselves on fire for causes far less than that of freedom. If we cannot find the mindset and motivation needed to fight a cold war, then how could we ever be prepared to fight a real one if it should come to us?

"Compared to war, all other forms of human endeavor shrink to insignificance. God help me, I do love it so."
General George S. Patton

The way to win a potential war is to not even think in terms of winning or losing like your enemy. But rather learn to love the fight itself and hope you'll be able to cause pain to the enemy for all eternity. There is nothing a government hates more than a never-ending war and never-ending financial losses. A mindset like this would create an opponent no one would want to go up against. Having the right mindset in war is the single greatest contributor to the outcome. War requires a *full* commitment, dedication of oneself, and an acceptance of giving that last full measure of devotion. Anything else is a waste of energy, time, and life. If the option of war is ever to be seriously considered, we must first have the proper mindset.

<u>What We Must Do</u>

We only seem to have the foresight of the upcoming election when we need to have the foresight to counteract problems 5, 10, 20, 50, and even 100 years from now. We must continue to do what we have seen work and avoid what doesn't. After sustaining many repeated injuries from our oppressors, let's follow our founders' blueprints while adding a modern touch. We can boycott, protest, vote, petition, organize and coordinate our efforts. We must stand up for what we believe and stand against what we do not at every chance we get. We must collaborate with one another. All ideas are worth mentioning and discussing. We must use the law to fight back against leftism and tyranny. Use their own laws, policies, tactics against them in an equal and opposite reaction. Question them. Question their authority, question their motives, question their ability to form a rational argument by playing the devil's advocate. Such as, are EVs more harmful than good? Could global warming if true be good? Any form of resistance possible. We must organize many boards of leaders, our wise and intelligent, those with some power and influence, to discuss the true state of our union nationally, regionally, state, and local. We must all get on the same page to have some form of division take place. How great would it have been if we had already established sanctuary for the police officers who needed to escape their hostile work environment during the defund the police/ BLM movement, as well as a sanctuary for the health care workers and military service members who refused the Covid19 vaccine mandates? What if we had a pre-established sanctuary for all in the most likely of scenarios? What if we started creating rightwing sanctuary cities for freedom and sanctuary from leftist oppression? We need to create a right-wing national emergency response organization, fully capable of restarting our government, economy, and military on every level in the event of a tyrannical takeover.

In this cold war, we can take steps to become economically independent through boycotting what we do not approve of, but also choosing to put our money in what we do approve of and favor. We can organize and build up a parallel economy as we have already started to. This includes companies and websites such as Parallel economy.com, woke alerts, public sq, parlor, rumble, Truth social, X, patriot mobile, Tusk, Black Rifle coffee, Jeremy's chocolate, Ultra-right lager, coign.com credit card, mammoth nation.com, and Gab.com just to name a few early participants.

We can flee oppressive states for a better one, but if we do, we are giving that state up to tyranny, and if we do, we will eventually see two different nations emerge. Or maybe many. If you are in an overwhelmingly leftist district or state, consider it lost and get out before it's too late.

Whatever we do to resist, we must be unified in our efforts, and we must stand up for one another. It would be all too easy for a government to oppress its citizens if individuals had to stand alone in their noncompliance. They will exterminate any resistance if it's a slow trickle instead of a flood.

The Catalyst

If a war broke out, how could it have been started? Would it be a Boston massacre leading to a Lexington and Concord? Would it be a Bleeding Kansas leading to a Fort Sumter? Would it be a Waco TX escalation?

What we do know is whoever controls how the war starts, most likely controls how it ends. Being prepared for a war in the beginning will determine how it begins, and how it begins usually determines how it will end. Like a Jenga tower, which blocks are pulled determines the way the tower tips. If resistance starts in an uncoordinated panic, such as a response to a second lockdown or firearm band, it would be quelled quickly as previously stated, individuals are easy for a government to overpower.

There are multiple possible tyrannical government take over scenario's history has revealed to us. All of which evolve and unfold at a different pace.

The first is a "Frog in boiling water" scenario- a gradual power grab process that evolves too slowly to be noticed or of a concern to most citizens until it's too late for them to do anything about it. Citizens are "boiled to death" before they have a chance. It is difficult for one to be agitated enough by a slow assault on their freedom to want to take desperate measures.

The second is a "False start" scenario- a scenario in which citizens take notice and start to react to their loss of freedom but they react individually or in small groups and are easily dealt with before their resistance gains too much momentum. The tyrannical government rids society of *problem* citizens one problem at a time. The rebellion gets a "false start."

The third is a "Snowballing" scenario- a scenario that favors a rebellions chance of success. Tyranny escalates its power grabs quickly but not too fast for citizens to take notice, protest, organize, plan, coordinate, and execute effective measures of resistance. Tensions escalate until blood is spilled. The rebellion starts out strong enough to survive the initial action from the government to quell the resistance. The government's actions against its citizens and news of the rebel's effectiveness only fuels the momentum of the rebellion.

The fourth is the "Powder keg" scenario- This is an instant explosive event scenario that will rapidly evolve into full out chaotic warfare. This scenario also favors the rebels, but the lack of time allowed for the rebel forces to organize, plan, coordinate, and execute effectively against the tyrannical government, will end up drastically hurting the rebellions chances of success.

War and street violence are inevitable if we continue to take no action to separate and rule ourselves our own way. But if we are wise and give the matter our complete and careful attention, we can in effect have a controlled explosion of sorts. Our fellow Patriots in 1775 knew that whichever side had the most control over when, where, and how the war started, would have more control over the events to follow. Thus, giving them the upper hand throughout the war and most likely resulting in their victory. People who feel like they are in hell tend to fight like it. The ghosts of freedom will forever haunt the tyrants of this world.

Chapter 9
THE ARGUMENT FOR A LOST CAUSE

Incoming generations always seem to view the problems and lessons of the past as insignificant, obsolete, or not applicable to them or the modern world. However, reality isn't like updating computer software, out with the old in with the new. Fundamental concepts and principles of the past remain just as important and applicable today as ever before.

Many today have tried to argue against any idea that free people must defend that freedom from any and all, at all costs. These arguments usually center around guns.

Arguments against the 2nd amendment in the U.S. Constitution include:

#1 "Our founders weren't talking about 'military style' weapons." "Such as cannons."

All weapons were and are military weapons if the intent to use them as such is there.

In the Revolutionary War, there was no difference between military and civilian weapons. The term "military style weapon" seems to have been made up. As far as cannon ownership goes, you could own one with little to no issues and can still own one today. And if they mean automatic weapons, they are already illegal for most to own.

<u>#2 "Our founders could never have imagined the weapons we have today when they wrote the 2nd amendment."(Modern weapons) (multiple rounds)</u>

I have to chuckle at this argument as our founders certainly understood innovation in military weapons. They witnessed the most rapid evolution of one of the greatest impacting military technologies of all time; the firearm itself. From its beginning, the firearm was extremely primitive compared to the finely tuned rifle it had evolved into by the time of our founding fathers. That aside, the premise for this argument is flawed to begin with, as it detracts from the whole point our founders were trying to get across to us in the first place. As Alexander Hamilton said, "The best we can hope for concerning the people at large is that they be properly armed." But properly armed for what? Properly armed for what they just finished doing. Properly armed for the possibility of engaging in an armed conflict against your own government's military when it seeks to oppress its people so to put the people back in charge of their own freedom and way of life. As Thomas Jefferson said, "The tree of liberty must be refreshed from time to time with the blood of patriots and tyrants." It's almost as if our founding fathers understood human nature and its perpetual self-serving lust for power.

<u>#3 "You are ignorant to believe American citizens could actually win a war against a government that has tanks, drones, fighter jets, and nukes."</u>

"The secret is not new weaponry; wars may be fought using weapons… but they are won by men. It is the spirit of the men who follow and the man who leads that gains the victory." General George S. Patton

It's true that no one is any kind of match against the U.S. military's technology, arsenal, or capability. However, the results of wars are not solely determined by these factors alone. The war in Afghanistan being the most recent and most accurate example of how a fighting force with little more than rifles took on the modern U.S. military for 20 years and ended up not only winning but better off than before. The Soviets had a similar fate in Afghanistan as well. The U.S. had the same fate in the Vietnam War. And what about our own war of independence? At the beginning of the war, we were nothing. Barely organized, no fighting force, no navy, no money, nothing.

Or what of other nations' wars for independence when they as well were "out gunned"? What of the countless battles in history that were won by strategy and tactics rather than technology and might? History has shown us that especially when it comes to a mighty and advanced fighting force occupying a nation, it usually doesn't end well for the occupiers. Remember, rebellions are often self-feeding. As in, the more enemy killed the more supplies, tech, and weaponry obtained. The oppressors end up unintentionally funding and supplying the rebel forces they are fighting against. Very importantly as well, a rebel force doesn't actually have to win, they just have to hold out long enough for the oppressors to give up and turn back. "You shouldn't underestimate an enemy, but it is just as fatal to overestimate him." General George S. Patton

High tech and mighty conventional weapons only work well in conventional warfare. Nukes have only been used at one point in war against one opponent, and for good reason. If the US government won't use it on an enemy, would they use it on their own people on their own soil? Especially when winning the hearts and minds of their people is the primary focus. Who would they even nuke? In unconventional warfare, the enemy isn't standing on their side of the battlefield. They are blending in with the general population. This also means the use of drones, tanks, and fighter jets would also be largely ineffective against rebel forces.

As far as technology in general goes, we have seen first-hand in Afghanistan how slow tactics and technology are implemented through government bureaucracy vs how quickly new tech and tactics are implemented by small fighting forces on the ground. Our forces struggled to keep up the implementation of IEDs, IEPs and enemy tactics in both Afghanistan and Iraq. In America, we have some of the most creative and innovative minded individuals in the world.

Our Military

This argument that we couldn't win against our military is also assuming that our whole military would be against us. The division in this country is largely political and approximately a 50-50 split. So, if the military is divided in the same way, (even though we know it's mostly conservative) it would be safe to say a large number of service members would be loyal to the rebels. Service members pledge to defend the US Constitution and obey the orders of the President of the United States and the officers they serve under. But what if the orders they receive, and the defense of the US Constitution contradict each other?

The military is also struggling with finding new recruits. New studies have shown that the majority of young people are significantly overweight and unfit for military service. Not to mention the complete lack of enthusiasm of young people to serve their country. Among the many character flaws contributing to their lack of service enthusiasm, they have also witnessed the Afghanistan withdrawal and know of similar failures in Vietnam. This leads them to the realization that those in power care little for those who give everything of themselves in service to their country. This also has made a lot of anti-government veterans. Having veterans on the side of the rebels would be crucial to a rebel victory. In the Revolutionary War, many of the leaders, officers, and soldiers had previously served the British crown in the king's army, including George Washington himself. Over time, their own military became more and more foreign to them and less recognizable. Today, we are now seeing our military cater to the culture of one political party instead of remaining neutral and focusing on combat readiness. At the same time, abandoning its appeal to Patriots and those who have value for loyalty, duty, respect, selfless service, honor, integrity, and personal courage. This leads to the military becoming less and less recognizable to many

Americans and veterans. Many service members may begin to wonder if the uniform they wear still means the same thing that it once used to. As history has shown us, when people can no longer recognize their own military, war is inevitable.

Furthermore, in this theoretical second civil war scenario, rebel forces may be smart enough to wait for a more opportune time to consider their rebellion. A time when the military is spread thin. As in preoccupied with yet another long drawn-out, costly conflict overseas. This would strain the military supply chain as well as troop numbers. Through wokeism in our military, we are essentially replacing our actual soldiers with just federal employees with rifles. The ancient Greek Spartans showed the world what can be done when actual soldiers fight a much larger force of just conscripts.

The Numbers

"It is not in numbers but in unity, that our great strength lies; yet our present numbers are sufficient to repel the force of all the world."

Thomas Paine

In the Revolutionary War, less than 3% of the colony's population was willing to fight for the cause in the Continental Army and militias. It is estimated there are currently between 200 and 300 militias and paramilitary organizations across the United States, with 15-25,000 members. The nation has 16.5 million veterans. Making up 6.4% of the US population. The United States military members currently are about

0.5-1% of the nation's population, and our nation is politically split approximately 50-50.

<u>A Purely Hypothetical</u>

For the sake of argument and curiosity, let's continue to explore a purely hypothetical yet likely scenario in which a nation much like the modern United States, finds itself with a tyrannical government which triggers a rebellion. How could these rebels fight, and win against their own tyrannical government? For an example, let's use the current political set up of the United States in this scenario. With the leftist extremists taking power and becoming the tyrants, and those on the right become the freedom fighting rebels. We see the odds are strongly in favor of the rebels, assuming all the correct preparations are made before war breaks out. With economic preparations of separation already made, the rebel army will have secured its future funding. Although the numbers are split 50-50, the rebel forces will have very obvious advantages. The rebels would have almost all of the civilian owned firearms with right wing individuals being very pro 2nd amendment. Most hunters, police, military, and veterans would side with the rebels, and be trained shooters. Firearm and munitions manufacturers are obviously pro 2nd amendment, giving rebels their own war factories at the start of the war. The political geography of the United States would give the rebels their greatest advantage. With major cities as leftist strongholds, and the rest of the nation secured by rebel forces, the war would be all too simple for the rebels. Like a small archipelago of tyranny lost in a sea of freedom fighting rebel forces, the war would be over before it begins. All rural communities are self-sustainable, even many rural households are as well. Being able to function with limited logistics. This rural nation would have within it all of the interstate transportation, farms for food, mines for war materials, oil for fueling the economy and war efforts. Many of the nation's power plants and utility stations are also found in rural areas. All of these factors combined would give any rebel force the edge needed to assure their victory.

It would be an embarrassing shame if such a force with such odds in their favor didn't attempt to secure their freedom and future. If they don't, never would an oppressed people have been handed such advantageous circumstances, and yet failed to have the minimal necessary courage needed to take action. Resistance fighters during World War 2, had nothing to fight with and few numbers, but they stood up to not one oppressor, but all the Axis powers. They fought back against tyranny, not because they thought they had a chance, but because as long as they lived, it was their duty to punish tyranny any way possible. A zero percent chance of success is enough for any free man to stand and fight.

The Eleventh Hour

How would such a war scenario begin? The onset of the war will most likely be a slowly evolving cold war with a slow escalation. With continued cultural divide, weaponization of our legal system, and an escalation of violence and street incursions. We simply have it too good in this country and are so far removed from most of the hardships of reality that too many people will remain calm and complacent until the last shred of hope and freedom disappear. By that time, it will be too late to do anything peacefully about it. Lack of commitment and inability to recognize the severity of their reality has always been and always will be the biggest reasons why free people lose their freedom and hand over their country to tyrants. If the oppressors escalate their assaults on your way of life and your freedom, the threat doesn't disappear if you do nothing. They will take whatever ground that is easy to take. The only proper response for the oppressed is to match the oppressor's aggression. By this time, the oppressed will have protested as fiercely as possible and have been ignored time and time again. The time for settling issues through discussion and complaints is now over. It's time for actions and ultimatums. Time to completely deny the oppressors what they want, and for the oppressed to stop asking for what they want and just start taking it. The oppressed must separate themselves from their oppressors by any means necessary.

In the final stage, on the path to civil war, the law is weaponized to attack and eliminate political rivals. This creates a time of paranoia for the oppressed, and for good reason. Previously assembled militias or any other form of organized resistance need to assume they have already been infiltrated by federal agents. Organizations cannot risk compromised identities and communications. For this reason, resistance groups will benefit from being small in size in the beginning.

These groups must be centered on trust. Those who can't prove themselves to be reliable and trustworthy when all is well, cannot be relied upon or trusted when times get tough. When the war starts the most trusted can help plan, the next most trusted can fight, and the least trusted can obtain resources. Everyone else could be used to unknowingly provide intel.

This is a time for identifying the enemy or possible threats, as the same is already being done to the resistance. This is when spies become useful. Spying is quite simple and can be done by anyone. Information on enemy plans, intentions, technology, tactics, capability, strategy, positions, movements, and numbers can be used by a rebel group or shared between them to gain the advantage. Unlike conventional Intel gathering, this early non-centralized military force must rely on quantity of Intel rather than quality. Or many sources over trusted sources. With a poor line of Intel and communications, a group can use many sources of information to triangulate the truth.

"Spies are a most important element in warfare, because on them depends, an army's ability to move." Sun Tzu

When the peaceful, legal route fails, the only alternative route leads to violent conflict. Rebels become law abiding citizens by day, and agitators by night. Rebels must beware of government surveillance cameras that can be used to identify and locate resistance groups. Those in power hide behind their minions who are fighting in the streets. The rebels must hold them accountable for their repeated injuries to them. The politicians know they are a target and now hide behind police and national guard.

Protected more than ever before, the tyrannical elite now use emergency powers and their majority to fulfill their most radical and oppressive agendas and policies yet. The stage for an armed incursion with your own military and the next "Lexington" is set.

Zero Hour

A domino effect is caused when war is the mindset of a majority of people across the nation. When one hostile encounter goes too far, word spreads and pushes many to take drastic action in response. At this stage the oppressors will make full use of the law, making it their front line while using law enforcement officers as their soldiers. All attempts are made to keep order and quell any uprising. With enough momentum behind the uprising, it may be too late for the oppressors to stop it.

The uprising turns into a full out rebellion, forcing the military into asymmetric warfare within its own borders, and ranks. If the rebels are to win this hypothetical, the first focus of the rebellion would be to: gain loyalty, gain numbers, gain supplies, and gain territory. The best way to do all of this is to focus on gaining loyalty to the cause first. The local mayor, sheriff, police chief, even the local national guard command. Where a loyal command structure isn't, one must be created. Rebel forces must prioritize those giving the orders, and not waste time, effort, resources, and life on grunts that will not yield progress. Zero hour is the time for everyone to pick a side and take action. Police officers and military service members have the most crucial decision to make. Do they defend freedom and the constitution? Or do they obey their master's like "good soldiers"?

The oppressors will make full use of civilians that are loyal to them by using them to spy on their neighbors and turn them into the authorities. This, however, can also be used against them. Civilians loyal to the rebels can overwhelm the oppressor's information system and create false reports to make their oppressive neighbors look like the enemy. This will create an overwhelming and unreliable information system which just might be shut down for these reasons.

The media will no doubt become a propaganda machine against the rebels. They will make false and staged stories. When the war really heats up, they will go along with the militaries reports of blaming their own civilian collateral damage on rebel forces. It's extremely important for the rebels not to make enemy propaganda easy for them. Rebels must ensure zero loss of innocent civilian life, and if possible civilian property. Aside from the obvious emotional and moral reasons, this would at the least turn public support against the cause, stealing potential members and bolstering enemy ranks. If the government and media aren't already manufacturing stories like this, rebels would be wise not to gift them a story. Rebels must not act like terrorists and must act within the laws of war. Most of the war would be the fight for the hearts and minds of the general public. The media's stories, however, can be a way for rebels early on to communicate in a few ways. Rebels can have some idea of what other groups are doing, and when and where they are doing it. This will boost morale and motivate other groups. Secondly this helps groups share tactics, ones that work and ones that don't. Thirdly, a sort of check list is established, of which targets have been successfully destroyed and which have not. Fourthly, direction of attack, attacks may begin to take on a theme or pattern for others to follow creating a "hive mind" sort of coordination. Dates or events also play into this pattern. Communicating indirectly would be an absolute necessity with a resistance force of multiple unaffiliated smaller groups.

With rebel targets established, where should they start? As these previously assembled small groups of rebels are cut off from each other mainly for communication security and secrecy purposes, it would be best if each group would focus on its own "backyard." As in, "watch your lanes." Rebels must secure their own local area that is within their group's ability to secure. If all groups do this, a "front line" will soon be established, and groups will be able to unite to establish communications and eventually a standing army.

"Move not unless you see an advantage; use not your troops unless there is something to be gained; fight not unless the position is critical."

Sun Tzu

—*Tactics*

"Good tactics can save even the worst strategy. Bad tactics will destroy even the best strategy."

General George S. Patton

What tactics should be used? Hiding forces in the wilderness is not possible in modern day America. Drones and spy satellites would find them on day one and forming a standing army against a superior equipped and trained force would lose the war fast. Rebels must save the organized military for when significant territory has been secured. Instead, rebels must hide in plain sight. The oppressors can't kill an enemy they can't see. Operating on an individual or small group level would make it near impossible for the enemy to find rebels, intercept communications, or infiltrate a rebel team. Significant historical dates could also be used by all groups separated from communications to coordinate the day of attacks. Rebels would be able to operate indefinitely this way, fighting the war in effective and less obvious ways than open combat. A large number of independent groups all with the same idea and united in cause, would without a doubt have an effect on the enemy as if they were one large military force.

"Do not repeat the tactics which have gained you one victory, but let your methods be regulated by the infinite variety of circumstances."

Sun Tzu

Aside from secure communications, smaller fighting forces are also stealthy, mobile, and fast. They can disappear as quickly as they came. Especially if they learn to disappear by blending into the civilian population. The Achilles heel of a giant is its size. Rebels can use its strength against it. Such an enemy force will be obvious, hard to hide, and an easier target to hit. It would be slow to move, slow to improvise, slow to implement new tactics and strategies. It would be slow to send information back up the chain and must wait for information to come back down the chain. Its strength is in communicating with large numbers at any given time. But what if different types of attacks were happening to all different parts of its body at the same time? Or what if it's heavily relied upon Intel was feeding it all different reports simultaneously? What if the rebels fought like ghosts and appeared to be everywhere at once yet nowhere? Could the giant become disoriented? Confused? Leading to indecisiveness or impulsiveness? "Numerical weakness comes from having to prepare against possible attacks; numerical strength, from compelling our adversary to make these preparations against us." Sun Tzu

If the giant trips and falls, it falls hard. Its size can be used against it like the 7,000 Greeks did to the around 250,000 Persians at Thermopylae in 480 BC. There are many battles in which the size of an army wasn't as influential as intended, such as The Battle of Gaugamela on 1 October 331 BC with Alexander the Greats Greek army against the enormous army of the Persians, and many other battles of Alexanders as he knew the best way to defeat a giant was to cut off its head. Another great example, the battle of Cannae in 216 BC when 50,000 Carthaginians won against 86,400 Romans. Or the final battle during the Boudican revolt in 61 AD when 10,000 Romans won against 230,000 Celts. Just to name a few of the first great examples out of thousands of battles throughout history of how brain won over brawn.

Rebels must use intelligent, creative, and resourceful tactics to compensate for their lack of size, strength, and equipment. The ancient Greeks for example used the phalanx formation to compensate for their lack of numbers. Rebel forces throughout history have used ***hit and run guerilla warfare*** tactics, as well as targeting the enemy command structure, as done by Continental militias in the American Revolutionary War.
"Never let the enemy pick the battle site."

General George S. Patton

The ***terrain*** with each engagement can either be used in one's favor, or against them. This has been proven more than any other tactic throughout time. Thermopylae being the most famous, as well as Battle of Stirling Bridge in 1297, and the Battle of Morgarten 1315 are a few examples of how terrain can not only even the odds but help win the battle even when vastly outnumbered. Rebels must know what terrain works in their favor and what works against them, as well as what terrain works in the enemies favor and against them.

"We are not fit to lead an army on the march unless we are familiar with the face of the country, its mountains and forests, it's pitfalls and precipices, its marshes and swamps."

Sun Tzu

Ambush tactics have proven to be extremely successful in every war since the first. Ambushing the enemy may have become easier with the changes that have come with the modern landscape. A landscape perfect for directional explosives. More buildings for concealment, more bridges and overpasses for strategic strikes. An ambushed enemy traveling at higher speeds would take on greater damage. Same old tactic, new applications. The effectiveness of an ambush is amplified with use of terrain such as the Battle of Trasimene in 217 BC with the Carthaginians ambush of the Romans, or the Teutoburg Forest in 9 AD with the German tribes decimating the Romans.

Disadvantaged forces of the past have also resorted to the use of clever *traps*. Traps can also be used with terrain such as at the Battle of Loudoun Hill in 1307 with the Scots slaughtering the English after the English cavalry were stopped by a series of trench traps and spearmen. The Battle of Gate Pā in 1864 with the British defeated by the Māori, is another great example. Using traps and trickery that lead to the British unexpected defeat after the Māori disadvantaged the attacking British who had laid siege to the Māori fort for days. From spring traps to tank traps to explosive traps to the tunnels and punji pit traps used by the Vietcong in the Vietnam War. Anyone can build a trap with minimal resources and ingenuity. Shotguns are very common among gun owners today, and their shells are highly versatile for making many weapons and traps that may give rebel forces an edge in many situations.

Weather can also play a vital role in assisting rebels with gaining the upper hand if opportunities are seized. Weather may limit the use of certain enemy technology and equipment and can leave them virtually immobilized. Weather can assist efforts such as in the destruction of the Spanish Armada by the English in 1588 aided by high winds. Or Washington's retreat from Long Island in 1776 aided by heavy fog. The Russians were aided by extreme cold when Napoleon invaded in 1812, and again against the Nazi invasion in 1941.

Financial warfare comes with the realization that all things related to war or any individual's survival comes down to capital. As we've seen in Canada during the trucker's protest, a Dictator has the power to freeze the bank accounts and block aid to their political rivals. This has also been done many times before by Russia, China, and Sudan. Canada invoked the Emergencies Act and broadened the spectrum of Canada's "anti-money laundering and terrorist financing rules." This is a redefining of a law.

We often see corrupt politicians redefining or stretching definitions of laws to broaden their spectrum of control or spending. This is an extremely dangerous concept as it allows an individual with a lot of power to destroy an individual with little power. It makes it very personal as the government financially strangles the life out of your family. Governments know an individual is far less likely to try to resist powerful oppression if they stand alone, and that a people's only hope, to rid themselves of oppression, is to stand together. The government could even use its power to have individuals fired from their jobs and keep them from being rehired.

In war, rebels would be able to fight their more advantageous oppressors in a financial way as well. Using the opponent's pride against them, they quickly start losing the war financially without knowing it. A $4,000 smart bomb plus the cost of the delivery mechanism plus the cost to operate and maintain the delivery mechanism, just to kill a few enemy soldiers, is not a very cost-effective way to win a war. A brand new

$290,000 up-armored Humvee destroyed in an instant by an IED. All the high tech, all the man and machine power that a large military has, costs big money to build, repair, maintain, and operate. The cost to field and sustain a modern military compared to a local self-sustaining military force, is great enough to cause such a government to see a war as not financially worthwhile and end up withdrawing their forces. The war in Afghanistan for example, for the United States and the Russian invasion. The American Revolutionary War cost the British a fortune they already didn't have at the time. The empires of the past fell victim to this same problem. An empire's conquered territory had to financially be worth conquering and occupying. "There is no instance of a country having benefited from prolonged warfare." Sun Tzu

Snipers proved their effectiveness during the first world war and perfected their strategies during the second world war. Some of the most effective of these tactics was in the slowing down of advancing enemy forces that the Japanese became famous for. As American forces advanced on the retreating Japanese, they encountered a trail of hidden Japanese snipers tasked with the goal of killing as many Americans as possible while slowing down their advance to a crawl. American units would stop every time they encountered an enemy sniper and would not advance until the sniper was confirmed dead. Hiding up in a tree made them hard to see, and tying themselves to trees meant they wouldn't fall when killed, making it hard to confirm the kill. Such a strategy used today would be just as effective if not more so with every hunter in America owning a scoped rifle. If given urban concealment, and able to blend in with the general public, snipers could prove to be a game-changing fighting force.

Cyber warfare has proven to be highly effective in modern day warfare, and if the oppressors anger the wrong people with skill, the rebels may have another effective form of attack on the oppressors.

Multiple simultaneously coordinated attacks such as Operation Overlord during WW2, the 9/11 terrorist attacks, and the Tet Offensive in the Vietnam War have proven to give a disadvantage force an amplified affect of ***surprise attacks.***

An ***Army of distraction*** is a tactic that has been used many times in history in many different forms and still is used today even by smaller forces. A fighting force will spit in two using a smaller force to engage the enemy while the primary force moves in on the enemies flanks and rear undetected. This is often very effective as contact with the enemy often creates many linear thinkers in the heat of the moment.

A rebel fighting force would also greatly benefit from focusing on the bigger picture of their victories. As in focus on ***symbolic, motivational, and strategic victories***. A smaller and disadvantage force will have greater chances and greater effects on the war in this way. I would argue that Washington's victory at Trenton in the American Revolution is an example of all three.

—Civilian side

Having an organized fighting force would be less of a benefit and more of a disadvantage in the early years of the war. The main advantage of fighting a war as an unsuspecting citizen are the advantages that come from being undetectable.

While rebels would be worried about their organizations being infiltrated by the enemy, rebels would already be planted as infiltrators in all of the enemies' organizations. As ordinary citizens rebels would hold an optimal and strategic position at their source of employment where they would be highly effective. A sort of Trojan horse. Any way they could cost, hinder, delay or inconvenience the enemy would all add up to be a great help for the cause. Factory workers and anyone involved in the production and transportation of enemy military equipment and munitions, would have an obvious role to play. A loose bolt here a misplaced item there, a cut wire. Rebels could sabotage wherever, however, and whatever possible. All other sources of employment could be used to spy, gathering information whenever, wherever, and however possible. Low risk, minimal effort, great convenience and it would have a large impact on the battlefield and especially the war.

—Technology

The oppressor's technology is often more advanced than rebel technology, but rebel technology is often more creative and resourceful. Rebels can create technology to aid their battle strategies as well as use the enemy's technology against them. An example of this was demonstrated in the Battle of Agincourt in 1415 when the French army had the numbers and the latest tech in medieval body armor, the British used the muddy terrain as a trap for the French heavy weights to get stuck in, and then the British made use of their long rang primitive long bows. The overall goal being, make the enemies clear advantages obsolete or ineffective with the use of clever tactics.

A modern oppressor's military will without a doubt come with tanks. Tanks are without a doubt an impressive weapon of war, but every technology has a weakness. With a little clever precision targeting any technology's critical components, that technology will be rendered useless no matter how impressive it may be. A Tank requires a crew, an engine, fuel and munitions. If its treads are broken, the 8-billion-dollar war machine with the latest armor and weapons tech, becomes nothing more than a 60-ton paper weight. Many nations resisting Soviet occupation soon realized tanks are very ineffective in urban areas as their main guns are unable to be raised to the height of a tall building, making them an easy target to be leisurely attacked. During Desert Storm the Iraqi army knew its tanks didn't stand a chance against the American tanks that had the advantage of range, power, armor, and accuracy. So, they hid their tanks all around their cities, laying low and waiting for American tanks to pass by. Staying hidden, assured them of the first strike. Drawing the American tanks into the city took away their range advantage. Striking at close range equaled out their power, armor and accuracy advantages. American tanks took much unexpected damage, and many were in dire need of repair.

Clever tactics are often best implemented through the use of new technology. Necessity is the mother of innovation and desperation is the mother of creative military technology and techniques. It's not just those with great funding that are capable of creating new tech, new creative devices, or new adaptations of existing tech. This has been seen in our most recent wars through the use of IEDs, IEPs, and suicide drones. Some of the most effective technology has proven to be some of the *simplest*. Including Body armor, RPGs, mortars, and artillery. Suppressors have also been playing a vital role in the Russia/Ukraine war, allowing small groups of soldiers to be as undetectable as possible.

Camouflage is technology that can favor rebel forces. Ghillie suits are highly effective and often hand made. Rebels would be able to implement technologies such as these to the battlefield faster than government forces. The government oppressors would also have the challenge of implementing different camouflage to all the many regions of the country. Whereas rebel forces would already have camouflage specific to their region and would not be concerned with uniforms in the beginning of the war. The best camouflage, especially against drones, would be looking like an ordinary citizen in a crowd of ordinary citizens.

Disadvantaged forces of the past have often made use of *faking out* the enemy. Either through decoy vehicles, fake soldiers to cover a retreat, even fake trees to hide snipers in. "All warfare is based on deception." "…when we are near, we must make the enemy believe we are far away; When far away; we must make him believe we are near." "Hold out baits to entice the enemy." "Pretend to be weak, that he (the enemy) may grow arrogant." Sun Tzu

Tricks to fool the enemy have always proven highly effective. At the Battle of Longewala in 1971, 120

Indian soldiers and 4 aircraft held out against roughly 2,500 Pakistani mechanized infantrymen and about 40 tanks. With some barbed wire and a handful of mines, the Indians were able to create the illusion of a minefield that redirected Pakistani forces under fire into an area with soft sand that the tanks and armored vehicles became bogged down in. This is a great example of tricking your enemy in order to use the terrain against them.

Unassuming tech such as **GPS** can even be used to identify enemy targets to some extent. Rebels would be able to use road hazard markers to label the enemy on GPS for all rebel forces to see. **Remote controlled** weapons are cheap, accessible, and highly versatile and effective on the battlefield as proven in Iraq and Afghanistan.

Enemy **drones** would prove a challenge, but once again they can't hit what they cannot see. They cannot label a person as a target if that person hasn't first labeled themselves as a target. Disappearing into the general population once again proves to be a vital strategy. Rebels can just as easily obtain and use drones. They don't have to cost a million dollars to be effective. Civilian drone tech can be just as useful. This will give rebels aerial surveillance capability as well as targeting capability. Drones have proven to be very useful in the Russia/Ukraine war.

Unique forms of **transportation** that many rebels privately own will also aid the rebels. From snowmobiles to fishing boats, and small airplanes, all will be able to play an evolving and critical role in winning the fight. ATVs have been playing an unexpected critical role in the Russia/Ukraine war.

These forms of transportation contribute greatly through either ability, mobility, or being cost effective. All of which may help create new tactics as well. Technology has always and always will, reimagine military tactics and strategies.

—Training

No military tactic or strategy can be effective without the proper training. Rebels would have a great opportunity to gain more advanced training than most government troops and could begin training long before a war breaks out. Better training can make fewer numbers outweigh larger numbers on the battlefield. A property trained rebel soldier would be able to do many jobs and tasks. This could allow a small rebel group to seize more opportunities that present themselves on the battlefield. Governments forces are often too big, bureaucratic, and overly complicated for their own good. It wouldn't be too difficult to have them out trained, especially when most veterans would most likely join the rebels. At the Battle of Brownstown in 1814, 200 untrained American militia were attacked by 25 Native Americans. 100 Americans were either killed, wounded, or missing. The Native Americans suffered only one casualty. Training is arguably the most important factor in combat.

"Maneuvering with an army is advantageous; with an undisciplined multitude, most dangerous." Sun Tzu

Every individual, tactic, technology, and training would have an evolving role to play as the war evolves into more conventional war. Individuals would be able to work as an agent gathering invaluable intel on enemy numbers, locations, movements, vehicles, weapons etc. As well as locating and terminating high priority personnel and logistical targets. High priority personnel targets range from those commanding enemy forces to the oppressive elites in power. High priority structural targets include infrastructure and buildings used in any way to aid the oppressors. Disrupting and delaying enemy progress in any way would be critical. Veterans would also have an evolving role as they put their experience and MOS job training to use. Most MOS training would prove to be critical when the war evolves into more of a conventional war. Certain MOS jobs give Veterans the know how to defeat and defend against the same technology they were trained on. Some tactics would prove effective at one stage of the war but not another. Tactics must evolve with the current state of the war. Some technology might also prove effective at one stage of the war and not the other. Adaption is key with a rapidly evolving war, and smaller forces have always proved to be able to adapt faster than larger forces.

The End Game

If the rebellion has made it this far, the oppressors are losing. As the rebels gain territory the smaller groups join forces forming larger groups and taking more territory. Larger forces join other large forces, and a frontline is formed. This is when victory is in view and the rebels must push forward with everything they've got. Mistakes cannot be made, as a break in the line would be very difficult to fill. A mass coordinated offensive is necessary at this point to deal the final blow. Every major city of the oppressors would now be surrounded. Just like surrounding a castle, the enemies forces would now be divided, and all enemy supply lines are cut off. Surrender is the only move the enemy has left.

"We may take it then that an army without its baggage-train is lost; without provisions it is lost; without bases of supply, it is lost."

Sun Tzu

Should the war become drawn out, remember the Taliban lasted 20 years of American occupation in Afghanistan. How long could freedom fighters hold out for if not indefinitely? What does the end result of war matter if you've been given the opportunity to live, fight, and possibly die a free man? Remember, rebel forces don't actually need to win, they just have to hold out long enough for the oppressive regime to give up and turn back.

So could the second amendment allow for a victory of oppressed Americans over their tyrannical government? I think yes.

The American Patriots of the Revolutionary War thought their chances were slim at best from the start. Then they lost New York among many other significant losses and were in full retreat. But they endured defeat after the next, and they endured many sufferings at Valley forge. In the beginning when all hope was lost, the battle of Trenton gave them enough hope to see Saratoga which then gave them enough hope to see the British surrender at Yorktown. They won against a world giant with only three percent of the colony's population fighting.

"Let us therefore animate and encourage each other, and show the whole world that a Freeman, contending for liberty on his own ground, is superior to any slavish mercenary on earth."

"The time is now near at hand which must probably determine whether Americans are to be freemen or slaves; whether they are to have any property they can call their own; whether their houses and farms are to be pillaged and destroyed, and themselves consigned to a state of wretchedness from which no human efforts will deliver them. The fate of unborn millions will now depend, under God, on the courage and conduct of this army. Our cruel and unrelenting enemy leaves us only the choice of brave resistance, or the most abject submission. We have, therefore, to resolve to conquer or die."

General Orders July 2, 1776, Commanding General of the Continental Army, George Washington

CONCLUSION

"To be prepared for war is one of the most effectual means of preserving peace."

George Washington

No matter the fate of this great nation, no fate should ever perceive this great experiment as a failure of any kind. We've built the modern world, saved mankind from great evils many times, and have done many great things for humanity. Had the United States formed two thousand years ago it would without a doubt have survived up to present day. It's easy for a nation to exist for a thousand years when the world requires so little of it, and when its trials are presented to it so slowly over time. Today, the world has never demanded more from a nation, nor a nation expected to overcome so many trials so rapidly. If the United States of America should ever leave this world with only one lesson to give, let it be how to fight for freedom. We can't always choose how we die, but we can choose if we die a freeman or an enslaved one. We owe our ancestors everything and we have the greatest of responsibilities in preserving our nation. Benjamin Franklin when asked what kind of government he had helped to create, he replied, "A Republic Madame. If you can keep it."

War is something no one should wish for, but we must be prepared for it to save ourselves and our nation. We are losing the things that make this nation the greatest in the world. We have been losing the battle with big government leftism not just for decades, but for generations. We have witnessed the Exponential growth of this government dependency disease. The administrative state has grown beyond our founders' wildest nightmares and ***must not be allowed to continue!*** The final nail of big government in the coffin of freedom will be requested, voted on, and passed with the sound of the desperate masses applause as they ask their chosen savior of government to fix their desperate problems that more government caused in the first place. The leftists have been building an empire with our hard earn tax dollars, bleeding us dry, taking money from red rural America and giving it to blue urban areas to prop up their failing policies and line the pockets of the corrupt leftist elites.

We must act **now** if we are to prevent a war as the window of opportunity to do so is sure to close on us at any moment. With the change of a nation's culture comes the change of the nation's principles, justice, law, morality, and conduct. We have already lost too much ground through inaction to be able to retake. Leftism has proven to be Anti-American, anti-religion, and pro-anarchy as it attempts to unravel the fabric of our society.

Most leftists don't even know why or what they are protesting, nor would they have a great enough reason to even if they did. They take action in every way possible whenever possible. Then you have those on the right, who know exactly what they believe and why they believe it and have the greatest, most noble and legitimate causes a person could ever have, yet we remain idle, timid, docile and respond passively and sluggishly.

We are under attack from all sides; so, from all sides we must return fire. We need to take the fight to them in any and every way possible. Instead of the left always attacking and we always are reacting, we must initiate an offence. Instead of the left pushing their form of a "great reset", we must strategize our own form of a great reset.

Our founding principles ignored, our values dismantled, our government grows bigger and more corrupt, our hard earned money is taken from our paychecks, our states power over ruled, our economic prosperity is being held back, our technology restrained, our military weakened and corrupt, our faith is under attack, our freedom over our bodies health is taken from us, our innocent raped tortured and murdered, our families endangered, our criminals set free, our voices silenced, our people villainized, our right to bear arms quickly eroding from constant attacks. Division and confrontation are inevitable if we do nothing. If our founders didn't have the foresight for something perhaps it was the severity of our differences today, or the urban/rural split, or the complete loss of reason and decency, or the cultural acceptance of delusion. Whatever they foresaw or didn't foresee, they gave us the protection of the Constitution, the tools of freedom, and the capability of self-rule, for us to make whatever changes and adaptations necessary for our survival and prosperity. A truly free society is one that can learn from the past and implement necessary changes to better its future, instead of perpetually repeating history's mistakes and never growing to its fullest potential.

"But a Constitution of Government once changed from Freedom, can never be restored. liberty, once lost, is lost forever."

John Adams

Should we let the tide pull us out to sea or should we do the obvious and instinctual, and fight for our lives? In this world, war is constant, and for the preservation of freedom, ever more so. We can't sit on the sidelines and watch our nation crumble around us. The leftist infection is spreading throughout our nation's limbs. We must amputate to save our nation's body from the disease of tyranny. When the iron glows hot, it's time to hammer. The time to act is now. **For those of you who once responded to your nation's call to action, you are needed to answer the call once more.**

We have had enough! Enough of the madness and chaos, enough of the nonsense, the backwards and upside down, enough of the irrational, the absurd, the indecent, the disrespect. Enough of the tyranny, the corrupt government, the inaccurate representation, the laws from the non-elected of the administrative state, the bleeding dry of the taxpayer for irresponsible spending. Enough being pushed around, ignored, mocked, labeled and bullied.

We are the hard working, dedicated, overtaxed, law-abiding citizens of this country. We give of ourselves to our families, local communities, and our nation's society. Many of us have served our country, and we have sacrificed far too many of our nation's finest. ***<u>We the Patriots are owed a better America</u>*** ***<u>than this.</u>***

"We the people of the United States, <u>in order to</u> <u>form a more perfect union</u>, establish justice, ensure domestic tranquility, provide for the common defense, promote the general welfare, and secure the blessings of liberty to ourselves and our posterity, do ordain and establish this Constitution for the United States of America" Preamble to the U.S. Constitution

It's time to "form a more perfect union" once more.

A long time ago a book was written for the same reasons as these by the great Patriot Thomas Paine who stated, "I offer nothing more than simple facts, plain arguments, and common sense."

The law is being used as a weapon of tyranny. Legislating what non-harmful items an individual cannot buy, and what an individual must buy. "Hate crime" laws that aren't used to protect citizens but punish others who have different political opinions, and to outlaw freedom of speech and artistic expression. Using the law to financially enslave us through taxes to pay for reparations and the welfare of non-citizens and projects for other countries. Using the law to target good citizens doing the right thing while those in the wrong get away with their crime. Using the law against religious establishments and their right to assemble. Using the law of the Constitution in unintended construed ways. Using the law against life, taking the lives of the innocent. Using the law to outlaw freedom in the name of safety. To take away parents' rights over their children's education. To tear down and rewrite our history. To allow destructive protests with left affiliation and deny protest of the right. To attack political opposition through double standards. To legalize election fraud and deny their political opposition their candidate to reject votes they disapprove of. Laws to restrict and deny our second amendment rights.

There are two types of rebels; those that rebel to obtain power, and those that rebel because of power to obtain freedom. The former decides for themselves when the rebellion begins. The latter lets their oppressors decide when the rebellion begins. So, when does the rebellion begin? As Jefferson stated, **"When tyranny becomes law, rebellion becomes duty."**